THE *Sermon* OF SERMONS

CHRIST'S SERMON ON THE MOUNT

RAUL RIES

SOMEBODY
LOVES YOU

PUBLISHING
WWW.SOMEBODYLOVESYOU.COM

Carpenter's Son Publishing

The Sermon of Sermons: Christ's Sermon on the Mount
By Raul Ries

Copyright © 2022 by Somebody Loves You Publishing

Editor: Claire Wren

Cover Design: Donna McCartney

Requests for information should be addressed to:
Somebody Loves You Publishing
22324 Golden Springs Drive
Diamond Bar, CA 91765-2449
(800) 634-9165
mail@somebodylovesyou.com
www.somebodylovesyou.com

---

1. Ries, Raul 2. Calvary Chapel—USA 3. Somebody Loves You Radio—USA
4. Evangelist—USA 5. Practical Christian Living 6. Discipleship

---

Words or phrases in brackets are not part of the original text. They have been added for clarification.

This book was primarily edited from Bible studies on the Sermon on the Mount by Raul Ries and published by Somebody Loves You Publishing.

Printed in the United States of America

978-1-934820-32-2

DEDICATED TO

all blessed believers in Christ—
the Church.

My prayer is for us, as His disciples, to become salt and light
in a very spiritually dark and evil world. We have embarked
on a journey to follow the narrow road—the way the Master
has mapped out for us. May the words of Christ's Sermon
prayerfully change us into His likeness—to personify His
holy attitudes in and through our lives to others. Jesus is our
Master Teacher. I pray His instructive words will burn
in our hearts and rekindle the flames of revival.

CONTENTS

A Word from Pastor Raul

Imagine sitting on one of the green, rolling hills surrounding the Sea of Galilee as Jesus sat down, and His disciples gathered close to their Master. He opened His mouth and taught them. His disciples remained still—listening—learning. Jesus was the central figure among the multitudes about Him—they were there to hear from Him. His authoritative voice traveled reaching the scattered multitudes. Jesus' audience must have been transfixed as they, too, listened to His wise words.

These instructive words of Christ are known as the famous "Sermon on the Mount." This lengthy sermon trained Christ's disciples how they, as children of God, should live. Jesus' teachings are intended to mold and shape the character of His followers, give them the essentials of Christian living, develop right attitudes, and produce spiritual fruitfulness. As King, Jesus was making official pronouncements about His kingdom.

Disciples of Christ need training. How are they supposed to live their lives in a sinful, spiritually dark world that is so opposed to Christianity? How do believers in Christ cope with life's everyday worries? What do Christians do when they are cruelly persecuted, and people, even from among their own family members, hate them?

In Christ's Sermon on the Mount, these basic questions are answered. Jesus addresses situations that every believer in Christ will face. Jesus' discourse is simple and profoundly practical. Every disciple can apply the sermon's teachings to their lives, as they rely upon the Holy Spirit to enable them to live the Christian life.

While on this earth, followers of Christ have a high standard to live by. They are to aim to be perfect, as their Father in heaven is perfect. Jesus led His disciples by example. He is our Leader; we are to learn from Him and daily pick up our crosses and follow Him.

This beloved sermon has been passed down from generation to generation, captivating a new audience of Christ's disciples and anyone else who has an open ear to listen for His voice from among the multitudes living in this sinful world.

As you move through Jesus' timeless *Sermon of Sermons,* allow God to speak to your heart. Whether you are a brand new believer in Christ, a disciple who has walked with Jesus for some time, or even a person who is yet unsure of following the Master, listen and learn.

I pray as you study the Sermon on the Mount, you will apply all that Jesus has to say to your life, individually. Allow God to work tremendously in your life and become a blessed believer . . .

Raul Ries

THE SERMON ON THE MOUNT

MATTHEW 5:1-2

And seeing the multitudes, He [Jesus] went up on a mountain, and when He was seated His disciples came to Him. Then He opened His mouth and taught them saying...

As Jesus preached the Gospel, taught, and healed many people, His fame spread throughout the region of Galilee. His relatively short ministry of 3½ years would have a lasting impact on humanity. At this time, at the height of His popularity, the multitudes thronged Him. As always, His disciples, the called, followed Him.

On this one occasion, seeing the multitudes, Jesus went up on a green mount of rolling hills and sat down. Once seated, His disciples came to Him, and He taught them. Jesus began a long discourse—the famous Sermon on the Mount which includes the beautiful Beatitudes.

In Israel, it was sometimes customary for the teacher to sit and the hearers to stand. On this instance when Jesus sat down, it was not for His comfort; it was for the importance of what He was about to teach His disciples. Jesus' teaching could have been an official declaration. It may have been a way of showing He was King by making an official pronouncement about His kingdom. Amazing! Knowing this, we should pay even more attention to His words.

On the northeast corner of the Sea of Galilee, near the place thought to be where Jesus fed the five thousand (Matthew 14:13-21), His disciples drew close to Him. The multitudes also gathered around and listened to Jesus (Matthew 7:28).

It is a memorable place for those who have visited Israel. Every other year, I take a group of people to tour the land, and travel on these same

9

hills. Someplace near where Jesus taught this sermon, we all sit under the trees to study the Sermon on the Mount.

Jesus' disciples listened, eager to hear every word. He spoke straight to the hearts of His disciples the principles that would characterize them as children of His kingdom. There was such power and authority when He taught them. His words burned in their hearts and created an insatiable thirst to hear more.

Jesus wanted His disciples to pay close attention and really listen to His words. He was very precise in what He taught them. Jesus wanted them to learn the blessings of kingdom living as children of God—the standards and characteristics that should be evident in a disciple's life. His followers were to have transformed lives.

Jesus also corrected the Pharisees' abuses of the Law of God. These legalistic, Jewish, religious leaders added 613 commands to the Law of God which brought people under much bondage. When Jesus taught His disciples, He corrected the Pharisees' teachings by saying, *"You have heard that it was said to those of old...But I say to you..."* (Matthew 5:21-22). Jesus, in correcting the problems with their laws as taught by the Pharisees, showed His disciples a better way to live—through the law of love, grace and mercy.

Some people have mistaken the qualifications given by Jesus in the Sermon on the Mount for prerequisites in the Kingdom Age—which refers to living in the thousand-year reign of Christ on this earth. This is known as the Millennium period that begins after the end of the seven-year Tribulation period. It is spoken of in Isaiah 11:1-10 and Revelation 20:4-6. The Sermon on the Mount is *not* a reference to the Kingdom Age.

Jesus' followers are called disciples. The word *disciple* means "learner." As disciples of Christ, we are becoming more Christ-like, and His characteristics should become evident in our lives. God desires to mold and shape us to become more like Him. It is important to know that God has a purpose and a plan for each of us—for His glory.

Dietrich Bonhoeffer, a German evangelical preacher and theologian said:

> The life of discipleship can only be maintained as long as nothing is allowed to come between Christ and ourselves, neither the law, nor personal piety, nor even the world...[1]

Those who are truly Jesus' disciples have been born again of the Holy Spirit (John 3). They have the indwelling power of the Holy Spirit living within them (John 14:23, 25). When Jesus calls us to be His disciples, what does He expect of our lives?

> *...Jesus said to His disciples, "If anyone desires to come after Me, let him deny himself, and take up his cross, and follow Me. For whoever desires to save his life will lose it, but whoever loses his life for My sake will find it. For what profit is it to a man if he gains the whole world, and loses his own soul? Or what will a man give in exchange for his soul?"*

> MATTHEW 16:24-26

Those called to be Christ's disciples have to count the cost of becoming His disciples. We do not follow Christ blindly. We pick up our cross and follow in the footsteps of Jesus Christ. When you take up your cross, you are dying to self—self-denial.

An American preacher and gifted writer, A.W. Tozer, also gave Christians an important principle to consider:

> Discipleship is a call to me, but it is a journey of "we." Jesus of Nazareth always comes asking disciples to follow him—not merely "accept him," not merely "believe in him," not merely "worship him," but to follow him: one either follows Christ, or one does not.[2]

In your commitment to be a disciple of Jesus Christ, never get sidetracked from *seeking first the kingdom of God*. Hold lightly to the things of this world. As a believer, you are to be ready for heaven—real simple.

Most people make the mistake of living for this world, not for the next. Think about everything you have accumulated materially in this world; it will be left behind. The only thing that will last is what you do for Jesus Christ—period!

I believe with all my heart that the Church is not living the principles taught by Jesus in the Sermon on the Mount. Christians have not put Jesus' words to practice in their daily lives.

I hope through taking Jesus' teachings on the Sermon on the Mount to heart, believers' lives will begin to change, and a new revival will begin in the Church. These are the very words of Christ spoken to us. Revival can happen!

1

BLESSED BELIEVERS

MATTHEW 5:3-12

In Matthew 5:3-12, we find the Beatitudes that Jesus taught His disciples who were in training. In their discipleship He wanted them to fully comprehend what their attitudes should be as followers of Christ.

BLESSED ARE THE POOR IN SPIRIT — Matthew 5:3

> "Blessed are the poor in spirit, for theirs is the kingdom of heaven."

Jesus spoke to His twelve disciples and to those who were listening nearby, saying, *"Blessed are the poor in spirit...."* *Blessed* in the Greek language means "Oh how happy." In teaching the Beatitudes, the first characteristic taught was to be *poor in spirit.* Jesus was not speaking about poverty—not having bread, milk or other necessary groceries. He spoke of a spiritual bankruptcy.

Those who have a poverty of spirit come to God knowing there is nothing good in them. They realize they are sinners. Those who are spiritually bankrupt submit to God and, in humility, empty themselves as they realize that apart from God, they cannot do anything.

Jesus' words would mold and shape His followers' characters; they were not to think of themselves more highly than others. They were to look at themselves rightly and humbly in the eyes of God. Those people who were truly poor in spirit would readily receive Jesus' teachings and submit to the will of God.

The prophet Isaiah was a man who had the right view of himself. As he stood before the presence of God, he saw himself in the correct light:

> *"Woe is me, for I am undone! Because I am a man of unclean lips, and I dwell in the midst of a people of unclean lips; for my eyes have seen the King, the LORD of hosts."*

ISAIAH 6:5

As a disciple of Christ, think about the lesson Jesus is teaching you personally. It is important not to think more highly of yourself than others. Are you poor in spirit? Do you have the right view of yourself? Are you aware that you are to live your life in the presence of God—in the light of His holiness?

BLESSED ARE THOSE WHO MOURN — Matthew 5:4

"Blessed are those who mourn, for they shall be comforted."

Jesus taught the next Beatitude to those who listened. He spoke about people who truly mourned over their sins. What did Jesus mean? The word *mourn* means "true repentance." Those who inwardly mourn are really sorry for what they have done to grieve God. There is an inner conviction never to do that same sin again. They have a sincere change of heart and are truly repentant. I believe a person who is spiritually bankrupt—poor in spirit—will mourn over their sin in repentance. You cannot have one attitude without the other. The only way to be a spiritual person is to be a person broken over your sin.

We all are born with a sinful nature; our hearts are described as *desperately wicked* (Jeremiah 17:9). Our sinful nature can make it hard to be a Christian and live a righteous, moral life. Think about it. Parents do not have to teach their children to sin; that comes naturally because of their sinful hearts. Parents have a duty to teach their children what is good and right. They have to train them how to live their lives according to God's Word (Proverbs 22:6).

In fact, as parents train their children by teaching them the Word of God, they will be spiritually equipped to survive in this wicked world. As you train your children, always make it a point to teach them about repentance, mourning over sin, and about God's forgiveness. They need to know that Jesus will cleanse and wash them from their sin: *...the blood of Jesus Christ His Son cleanses us from all sin* (1 John 1:7).

I am acutely aware of my sinful nature. I have had so much anger and hatred in my heart. Even though God has forgiven me, I will never forget the sinful things I have done for the rest of my life. I cannot take back committing adultery. Even though Sharon has forgiven me, knowing how I have hurt my wife in the past, I still mourn over my sin.

Honestly, looking back over my life, I wish I had been pure. Yet I know I am in the place where God has me, only because of the grace and love of God—period. Christ has wiped away all my sins. Whenever the devil tries to condemn me, I know Christ does not condemn me:

> *There is therefore now no condemnation to those who are in Christ Jesus, who do not walk according to the flesh, but according to the Spirit. For the law of the Spirit of life in Christ Jesus has made me free from the law of sin and death.*
>
> ROMANS 8:1-2

God has been so gracious; He has forgiven me—fully and completely.

What did Jesus mean when He said that those who mourn shall be comforted? Jesus spoke of the Comforter—the Holy Spirit, the third Person of the Trinity. He is the only One who can comfort us (John 14:26-27). Those who truly mourn over their sin will be blessed by experiencing the peace and comfort of God. When anyone comes to

God in true repentance, God will forgive them—those who mourn will be comforted.

When someone mourns over their sins, God gives them an assurance that they are forgiven. God loves them. He has the best washing detergent—the blood of Jesus Christ—it gets rid of every crimson stain! God wipes out their sins.

Those who have been forgiven should show compassion toward other people, as God has had compassion toward them. In humility, they should never throw stones—words of judgment. In fact, knowing that God has forgiven them of their sins, they should be more forgiving toward others.

BLESSED ARE THE MEEK — Matthew 5:5

"Blessed are the meek, for they shall inherit the earth."

Remember, Jesus began the Beatitudes by teaching His disciples about spiritual bankruptcy, being poor in spirit, and mourning over sin. Jesus continued: *"Blessed are the meek, for they shall inherit the earth"* (Matthew 5:5). Meekness does not denote weakness. Those who are meek exhibit power under control. They are truly humble in the eyes of God. Consider the incredible promise given to the meek—they will inherit the earth.

Those who have an attitude of pride exhibit haughtiness, and they are completely opposite of those who are meek. This promise is not for them. Pride will keep people from hearing from the Lord. Christians need to look to Jesus as He becomes our example of humility; we are to model our lives after Him:

> *Let this mind be in you which was also in Christ Jesus, who, being in the form of God, did not consider it robbery to be equal with God, but made Himself of no reputation, taking the form of a bondservant, and coming in the likeness of men. And being*

found in appearance as a man, He humbled Himself and became obedient to the point of death, even the death of the cross. Therefore God also has highly exalted Him and given Him the name which is above every name, that at the name of Jesus every knee should bow, of those in heaven, and of those on earth, and of those under the earth, and that every tongue should confess that Jesus Christ is Lord, to the glory of God the Father.

PHILIPPIANS 2:5-11

Meekness is the spiritual power given to the believer by the Holy Spirit, who will enable them to surrender and humble themselves to God in obedience.

BLESSED ARE THE HUNGRY AND THIRSTY
— Matthew 5:6

"Blessed are those who hunger and thirst for righteousness, for they shall be filled."

Jesus taught the first three Beatitudes so His disciples could learn what attitudes they should exhibit. They are to be poor in spirit, mourn over their sin, and have humility—meekness. Then begins a natural process where a follower of Christ begins to have an insatiable hunger and thirst for righteousness. They desire God!

If a person desires true spiritual satisfaction, they will search for the truth of God. A person who does not know God will not hunger after Him—he cannot. Instead, he will indulge in himself. That person will think of number one, me, myself and I. It is not until people see who they are in the eyes of God—sinners—that they can go through the process of spiritual bankruptcy, repentance and meekness, to then hunger and thirst for righteousness. As this happens, they will have true spiritual satisfaction. They will be filled!

THE SERMON OF SERMONS

Even in the Church, selfishness and immorality have become a major problem. Christians are too full of "self." Believers should never seek satisfaction in other places, as they can only become complete in Jesus Christ. We are children of the kingdom of God, and we can only find fulfillment in Him.

If Christians remain greedy and selfish, there will be no satisfaction in anything they do. In fact, they will end up living very lonely lives. Many people who are selfish do not have any fulfillment. They continually look for something else to satisfy their lives.

Over the years, I have watched the life of my wife; she is such a giving person. Rather than allotting time for herself, she spends her life doing good and helping others. She is satisfied—fulfilled—and I can see the peace in her life.

Naturally, Christians *must hunger and thirst for righteousness*—God's righteousness. It is given to them so they can be right with Him. Believers cannot be righteous in themselves; they enjoy fellowship with God because of His righteousness. As Jesus' disciples, we can stand before Him in His righteousness.

BLESSED ARE THE MERCIFUL — Matthew 5:7

> "Blessed are the merciful, for they shall obtain mercy."

Jesus taught yet another important characteristic of a child of God—mercy. *Mercy* can be defined as "not getting what you deserve." Christians should show mercy and compassion toward the undeserving. It is never good to be judgmental or be gratified in seeing a person reap consequences to their sins. Think about it. Christ has shown mercy to you by forgiving you of all your sins, so do likewise—be merciful and forgive others. Ask God to make you merciful and forgiving of others.

Jesus taught on the subject of forgiveness further on in the Sermon on the Mount. He said:

> *"For if you forgive men their trespasses, your heavenly Father will also forgive you. But if you do not forgive men their trespasses, neither will your Father forgive your trespasses."*
>
> MATTHEW 6:14-15

In ministry, I was taught by Pastor Chuck Smith to always err on the side of grace—God's unmerited favor toward sinful man. I have found this principle to be true. I believe all of us one day will need someone else to show us grace. If you *lean to the letter of the law* and are harsh and rigid with people, without extending grace or mercy to them, then I believe the way in which you have treated others will have a natural way of coming back to you.

Jesus wanted the pious, religious leaders—the Pharisees—to learn about mercy. Jesus sat and ate with sinners and tax collectors. The tax collectors were despised among the Jews, as they unfairly exacted money from the people to line their own pockets. The Pharisees looked down upon them and indignantly asked the disciples: *"Why does your Teacher eat with tax collectors and sinners?"* Knowing the Pharisees' hearts, Jesus responded:

> *"Those who are well have no need of a physician, but those who are sick. But go and learn what this means: 'I desire mercy and not sacrifice.' For I did not come to call the righteous, but sinners, to repentance."*
>
> MATTHEW 9:12-13

Notice, mercy is found in the heart of Jesus—this is a true Beatitude of Christianity. The God of the Bible is merciful. In Micah 6:8, there are requirements given for those who walk with God:

> *He has shown you, O man, what is good; and what does the LORD require of you but to do justly, to love mercy, and to walk humbly with your God?*

How has Jesus ministered to you personally about showing mercy? Ask Jesus to enable you to do justly and extend mercy to an undeserving person.

BLESSED ARE THE PURE IN HEART — Matthew 5:8

"Blessed are the pure in heart, for they shall see God."

Another characteristic seen in followers of Christ is that they have pureness of heart: *"Blessed are the pure in heart, for they shall see God."* I love this Beatitude because disciples of Jesus Christ, having a pure heart, receive the promise that they will see God.

Pureness of heart speaks about having a single mind—your life is completely consecrated to God's will. In heaven, we are told: *They* [God's servants] *shall see His face, and His name shall be on their foreheads* (Revelation 22:4). Incredible!

How can your heart be pure when Jeremiah 17:9 states: *"The heart is deceitful above all things, and desperately wicked; who can know it?"* We cannot trust our hearts—we cannot. The only way to have a pure heart is to place your faith in Jesus Christ. Why? You are not made pure by your own righteousness, but by His righteousness—so important.

The Word of God is purifying. When you come to Jesus Christ, He cleanses you from all your sins and grants to you eternal life. Jesus gives you the amazing privilege to serve and love Him. He enables you to stand true to Him with a pure heart. The Apostle Peter perfectly explains this truth to us:

> *Since you have purified your souls in obeying the truth through the Spirit in sincere love of the brethren, love one another fervently with a pure heart, having been born again, not of corruptible seed but incorruptible, through the word of God which lives and abides forever....*
>
> 1 PETER 1:22-23

Jesus is the purifying Light of the World. He brings light into your life as He reveals Himself to you through His Word: *Your Word is a lamp to my feet and a light to my path* (Psalm 119:105). Your souls will be purified by obeying the Word of God.

BLESSED ARE THE PEACEMAKERS — Matthew 5:9

"Blessed are the peacemakers, for they shall be called sons of God."

Who are the sons of God? Those who make peace are called the sons of God. Peacemakers do not want to inflict pain. Instead of escalating a situation, they decrease it by making peace.

Being a peacemaker creates an atmosphere where you are showing the love and compassion of God toward others. In doing so, it helps you to mature and grow in Christ. The conditions of peace are godly love and forgiveness.

I remember the many times when I would go into Pastor Chuck Smith's office with difficult situations. I personally learned from Chuck, as I witnessed his lessons of forgiveness when he practiced them toward others. When people came against him, cut him up into thousands of pieces and spewed him out, Chuck forgave them! It was amazing! I asked myself, *How can Chuck do that?* He had a pure and peaceful heart, and having taught the Sermon on the Mount many times himself, he applied Jesus' teachings to the situations.

In the past, if any person would hurt me, I would want revenge; but I have learned it is best to leave these situations in the hands of the Lord. Besides, I am accountable to what I have read in the Scriptures. If I act revengefully, I know God will cause the situation to fall back on me, too!

Honestly, even in my marriage I used to hold on to grudges. Sometimes all night long or maybe a week or two, I would watch our marriage relationship decline. I learned how important it is not to hold on to bitterness or to be unforgiving.

Always make sure your heart is right before God, your spouse and other people; otherwise, how can you tell people about Christ if your heart is not right with Him? You cannot.

Victorian England's best-known Baptist minister, Charles Haddon Spurgeon, began preaching in 1850, when he was only fifteen years old. He became known as the "Prince of Preachers." Spurgeon gave this tremendous exhortation to believers:

> This very day, put aside from you all bitterness and all malice, and say one to another, "If in anything you have offended me, it is forgiven; and if in anything I have offended you, I confess my error; let the breach be healed, and as children of God, let us be in union with one another." Blessed are they who can do this, for *"Blessed are the peacemakers!"*

As disciples of Christ, walk closely to Jesus Christ and start applying this Beatitude to your everyday life.

BLESSED ARE THE PERSECUTED — Matthew 5:10-12

> "Blessed are those who are persecuted for righteousness' sake, for theirs is the kingdom of heaven. Blessed are you when they revile and persecute you, and say all kinds of evil against you falsely for My sake. Rejoice and be exceedingly glad, for great is your reward in heaven, for so they persecuted the prophets who were before you."

The reason Christians will often be persecuted is because they are living a godly, righteous life of holiness for Christ. People dislike it when you will not compromise. When you choose not to tell lies or cheat, and instead you decide to be honest, they get offended. Expect to be persecuted when you make a practice of what Jesus taught in the Beatitudes, but remember you are to rejoice despite the trials you may endure because heaven awaits you.

Be prepared to be put down and mocked by those in the world. People will despise you, saying, "You are too narrow-minded." Well, yes, we are! Why? Jesus Christ has taught us principles and characteristics that will cause us to be narrow-minded. We are to be kept on a narrow path to eternal life:

> *"Enter by the narrow gate; for wide is the gate and broad is the way that leads to destruction, and there are many who go in by it. Because narrow is the gate and difficult is the way which leads to life, and there are few who find it."*

> MATTHEW 7:13-14

Understand, you will be persecuted—Jesus said it. Paul the Apostle confirmed it: *Yes, and all who desire to live godly in Christ Jesus will suffer persecution* (2 Timothy 3:12). Believers will be persecuted; some will be martyred for Christ, especially in other countries where Christianity is not tolerated.

Sometimes you may be falsely accused, but God is in control. Do not let false accusations and insults eat you up like a cancer. Let things go otherwise the devil will use these situations to infect your heart and mind with bitterness. Leave it all in the hands of the Lord.

Whenever you are doing what is right, people will criticize and oppose you. Even if they become angry and annoyed, you have to make a stand for righteousness' sake. When people come against you, always stand for truth. God is your Defender!

Christians will be persecuted for Jesus' sake, not for their sake, but for what they are doing for Christ—everything they do for the name of Jesus. When you are living the right way, people will persecute you and say all manner of things against you. However, what should be your reaction? *Rejoice and be exceedingly glad, for great is your reward in heaven!*

Christians, we are in good company. In Hebrews 11-12:1, you will find a *great cloud of witnesses*—the saints of old who have gone to heaven before us. We can learn from the faith of the patriarchs and saints who endured severe trials—Abel, Enoch, Abraham, Sarah, Rahab, Gideon, Barak, Samson and Jephthah. Then there was David, Samuel, all the Prophets and saints—believers in Christ. If the ungodly persecuted the prophets and the disciples in the New Testament, will you not be persecuted? Persecution has happened in times past, it is happening now, and it will continue well into the future. Think about it. People persecuted Jesus, the Son of God, and they will persecute you!

We are the disciples of Jesus Christ in the 21st century! The disciples who lived during the life of Christ opened the Church age, and we are closing the Church age. You can rejoice in persecution knowing that God is using you to be a light—a great influence in a spiritually dark and thirsty land. The reward for true believers is heaven. One day you will see Jesus face to face in all His glory!

2

SALT AND LIGHT

MATTHEW 5:13-16

Christians are the salt and light of the earth! They are a purifying factor in the world and bring light where there is darkness.

THE SALT OF THE EARTH — Matthew 5:13

> "You [believers] are the salt of the earth; but if the salt loses its flavor, how shall it be seasoned? It is then good for nothing but to be thrown out and trampled underfoot by men."

I believe Christ's depiction of us as the salt of the earth perfectly relates to our call to evangelism. In His authority, Jesus established our influential power to share the Gospel with everyone in the world. Knowing the Word of God, we can tell others about future, biblical events and give people the truth concerning eternal life. We are to be a compelling witness before the world.

In Israel, the Dead Sea is full of salt. It is never wise to get the sea's water into your eyes—it will burn. When stepping out into the water, because of the high salt content, you can slowly lean backward to float on top of the water and literally read your newspaper!

Think about salt for a moment. In biblical days, as well as today, what was salt used for? It was used for seasoning and as a preservative. In that culture, people had no refrigeration, and in such a hot climate, meat would quickly rot. In meat markets, salt would be rubbed into the meat as a preservative so it would not spoil. Salt is a very powerful mineral—it has purifying properties. Saline solution is still used today because it helps heal wounds by keeping the area free of infection.

Charles Spurgeon describes our Christian effectiveness:

> Followers of Christ, "Ye are the salt of the earth." You help to preserve it, and to subdue the corruption that is in it.

As a Christian, and as the salt of the earth, are you a person of spiritual influence? Are you a seasoning factor to this corrupt world? Does your life have preserving and purifying qualities?

Through our Christian witness, we should be drawing people to Christ. If we are to be effective, people need to see a marked difference in our lives, especially our family members and friends. Can they tell that you are a completely different person from who you were in the past? Can they taste you as the salt of the earth?

This analogy applies not just to individual believers, but to the Church—the body of Christ. The Church is to be as salt throughout this entire world. Yet if the Church loses its flavor, its influence is of no value; it has lost that purifying and preserving ingredient of salt. Having no effect, the world will triumph over the Church and trample it underfoot. Instead of the Church gaining ground, it will lose ground.

Even though churches are full, many people attending church are not spiritual people. In the congregation there are people like Achan, who tried to hide his sin (Joshua 7:19-25). Remember, a little leaven—sin—will leaven the whole lump—the Church (1 Corinthians 5:6). Every time a leader or any believer falls into sin in a local church, the enemies of God mock. What a shame it is when Christians bring a bad name to Christianity.

Another natural quality of salt is it creates a thirst. Is your life creating a spiritual thirst in the lives of other people so they can come to know

Jesus as their Savior? It is important to answer this question and realize who Christ has declared you to be—the salt of the earth.

As we continue to meditate over Christ's profound sermon, may God continue to change our hearts and attitudes so that we can become a strong influence as citizens of the kingdom of God. It is His Church— we are His people. We need to be the salt of the earth in light of Christ's soon return.

THE LIGHT OF THE WORLD — Matthew 5:14-16

"You are the light of the world. A city that is set on a hill cannot be hidden. Nor do they light a lamp and put it under a basket, but on a lampstand, and it gives light to all who are in the house. Let your light so shine before men, that they may see your good works and glorify your Father in heaven."

Jesus said to His followers, *"You are the light of the world."* This is an intense statement. Jesus used light as a metaphor so His followers could easily understand who they were in this world. Christians reflect Christ! In this spiritually dark world, people should see them as lights shining. As children of the light, they are a light to all those in the darkness.

Christians shine! They are the light of the world! That is the Christ-like life. Jesus spoke of our relationship with Him when He said: *"I am the light of the world. He who follows Me shall not walk in darkness, but have the light of life"* (John 8:12). Christians are no longer in spiritual darkness; they live in the presence of His light.

Consider the incredible benefits of walking in the light: *But if we walk in the light as He is in the light, we have fellowship with one another, and the blood of Jesus Christ His Son cleanses us from all sin* (1 John 1:7).

The Apostle Paul shared another truth of our new transformation: *For you were once darkness, but now you are light in the Lord. Walk as children of light* (Ephesians 5:8). Those called to follow Christ are children of the light, and they can no longer continue to live in darkness—on a path leading to eternal destruction.

Paul went on to say in Ephesians 5:11: *And have no fellowship with the unfruitful works of darkness, but rather expose them.* The Apostle made a clear distinction between light and darkness: *You are all sons of light and sons of the day. We are not of the night nor of darkness* (1 Thessalonians 5:5).

Light illuminates and extinguishes the darkness. Everyone practicing evil hates the light. How are evil deeds exposed? The light! Jesus declared: *"I have come as a light into the world, that whoever believes in Me should not abide in darkness"* (John 12:46). Yet there are those who would rather remain in the darkness. Why? Jesus made known the reason: *"And this is the condemnation, that the light has come into the world, and men loved darkness rather than light, because their deeds were evil"* (John 3:19*).*

At this present time, are you still walking in darkness?

I have found that most Christians who are living a life in the darkness are failing to read the Word of God, pray and fellowship with other believers. It could be they are still hanging around with their ungodly friends, and as a result, they find themselves compromising with them.

The world remains in darkness, but we have received the light of Jesus Christ. Remember, as Christians we are to be *a city that is set on a hill*—a witness for Christ.

A City on a Hill

Have you ever seen bright lights miles and miles away, up on top of a hill in the darkness? That is what a Christian's light is—a light on top of a hill that cannot be hidden.

When I first went to Israel, I looked over the Sea of Galilee from my hotel window at night, and in the dark distance, I could barely see a couple of lights flickering in Capernaum. At present, the cities in Israel have developed so much that now as I look out across the Sea of Galilee, I see bright lights shining in all the cities of Capernaum, Canaan, the Gadarenes and Tiberius. Imagine the incredible power of light!

As you enjoy intimate communion with God, you will be a continual flow of light in the darkness. Charles Spurgeon gives perfect insight into why we need to shine:

> The Bible is not the light of the world, it is the light of the Church. But the world does not read the Bible, the world reads Christians! *"You are the light of the world."*

Christians will blaze as lights in the midst of this world's chaos. That is why every believer is encouraged to:

> *Do all things without complaining and disputing, that you may become blameless and harmless, children of God without fault in the midst of a crooked and perverse generation, among whom you shine as lights in the world...*

> PHILIPPIANS 2:14-15

That is a great responsibility! The light penetrates the darkness. Light dominates. That must be our strong testimony.

A Light on a Lampstand

Jesus spoke of lit lamps being place on a lampstand. In Israel, a lampstand was a very familiar term. Within the Jewish tabernacle was a golden, fashioned lampstand—the Menorah. Seven lamps filled with olive oil were placed on this lampstand and the wicks were lit. Light illuminated the tabernacle all evening, until the morning.

People in Israel were familiar with the common clay lamps that burned olive oil. When these lamps were lit, they would be placed on a stand to give as much light as possible to their homes. This picture would have come to the minds of those listening to Jesus' words. In simplicity, Christ, the divine Light of the World, has given the light of life to our human lives. In turn, as His followers, the light we bear should be placed in a higher place where it can be used to its maximum illuminative power. A light is never to be hidden—obscured. Our light should shine, not only before the Lord in purity of life, but to attract people to Christ so they can be delivered from the darkness of this wicked world.

Light attracts. Have you ever noticed that light naturally attracts gnats, flies, moths, and an array of other pesky insects? When we become light, people will naturally be attracted to us. People who are inquiring about Christ may ask, "How do I come to the light?" As we are in the light, we should know the Word of God and be able to give them an answer.

Never hide your light! The world is in need of your light! Otherwise, people will continue to stumble in the darkness. People's minds and hearts are filled with darkness and violence. As Christians, we know how to function in this dark world, but spiritually speaking, those who do not know Christ are walking in total darkness—they cannot see until they receive the light of Christ. They are dead in their sin, and Satan keeps them blind:

> But even if our gospel is veiled, it is veiled to those who are perishing, whose minds the god of this age has blinded, who do not believe, lest the light of the gospel of the glory of Christ, who is the image of God, should shine on them.

> 2 CORINTHIANS 4:3-4

Light has life-giving qualities. If a person walks into a dark room, they naturally try to find the light switch. Once they find the switch and turn it on, the darkness is immediately gone. That is exactly what Christ has done with each one of us individually; those born again of the Holy Spirit of God have the light of life! They have turned on the light in their lives!

Light Bearers

The Church is to be a light in this world. With the coming of the Holy Spirit at Pentecost, the Church was empowered to be a light-bearer of the testimony of Christ. If that is so, why has the Church over the ages become dim? I believe sin in the Church diminishes the light, and the Church loses its effectiveness—so sad.

Christians cannot compromise. Believers need to obey the Word of God. They have knowledge of the Light—Christ. According to the Scriptures; they are not ignorant or blind. Believers who are playing with sin need to repent! They know what is right and wrong and simply need to turn on the light switch—reflect Christ to the world.

When God's Word is taught in any church service, people listen, and they become responsible for everything they hear. Christians cannot contradict God's Word in their lives. Believers need to be careful in what they say and what they do, how they walk, and how they act— there are no excuses. Once the light is turned on, they are liable. When a believer has experienced Jesus, the Light of the World, and has gone back into the darkness, they cannot really get away from the Light.

Christians need to let their lights shine in the world so that they draw people to God's heart. There are a lot of people perishing, including those in our families. They need to see a true transformation—the change that comes by being born again of the Holy Spirit. We became a new creation in Christ Jesus, and we are now being transformed day by day:

> *But we all, with unveiled face, beholding as in a mirror the glory of the Lord, are being transformed into the same image from glory to glory, just as by the Spirit of the Lord.*

> 2 CORINTHIANS 3:18

Believers should be careful not to stumble people by saying they are in the Light when people see them walking in darkness. We do not need to preach to people, but we need to live a life that radiates Christ before them. We want people to know the Eternal Light—Jesus. The world is so full of darkness, and people are looking for hope! If the Church cannot bring them hope, then what can we give to them?

Our light becomes dim when we sin against God—it is of no use. A light is not to be hidden. Everyone should be able see it, and as it shines, lives are brought to Christ. When people see the Light in us, they will ask, "How can I come to know Christ?" They will be attracted to the brightness of our light. It is so important for us as a Church to really be the light of the world—to be a light that shines far above the wickedness of this world for everyone to see.

Let Your Light So Shine

To be a light to this world really goes back to all the previous verses in Matthew 5. People need to see the Christ-like attitudes and characteristics in a child of God's life. It is only when believers live according to the Beatitudes Jesus taught them that they will shine as lights in this dark world. They will glorify Him.

Look at the people around you; are they glorifying God because you are shining the light of Jesus? God the Father should be glorified by the life we live. We are light—it is within us! Jesus, the Light of the World has been poured into our lives—it is amazing.

Wherever the Lord has placed you, as you shine, people see your good works. Let your light shine in order to stir men to glorify God the Father and Jesus Christ—not yourself. Through our lives, God will get the glory: *Not to us, O LORD, not to us, but to Your name give glory because of Your lovingkindness* (Psalm 115:1 NASB). For all believers, this is our primary aim—glorifying God.

Everlasting Light

Think of how important light is to this world. Without the sun's light and heat, our planet would be lifeless. Nothing is more useful and necessary in human life than light. We cannot live without it. If there was no light from the sun, there would be no life on earth. The world would be cold and in darkness. The sun's light reflects on the moon to give us light during the night. Light travels through space at just over 186,000 miles per second. A beam of light takes only about one second to reach the surface of the moon. That is incredibly fast! God created the sun to bring forth life from the earth, to give man light during the day, and the moonlight at night for as long as the earth endures.

Have you ever walked into a dark cave without a flashlight? It is an eerie darkness, so dark that if you held your hand in front of your face, you would not even be able to see it. Jesus taught that any person who does not know Him, is walking in the darkness. It is the worst darkness you can ever imagine, as it will lead you straight to hell—into pitch blackness—where the worm never dies and there is gnashing of teeth. Those who are cast there will never see the light again. They will be eternally separated from the Light of the World.

Jesus encouraged all who are lost in the darkness: *"Awake, you who sleep, arise from the dead, and Christ will give you light"* (Ephesians 5:14). Listen—rise from the darkness and come into His Light. Christ illuminates the path to repentance. Follow Him and you will no longer be in bondage to sin—no longer condemned to hell—and you can expect to go to heaven. I love that!

For the Christian, when they die and take their last breath, they will be in the presence of Everlasting Light. Think about it! The Lord will be to you an everlasting light:

> *"The sun shall no longer be your light by day, nor for brightness shall the moon give light to you; but the LORD will be to you an everlasting light, and your God your glory."*

> ISAIAH 60:19

God is Light. He clothes Himself with light:

> *O LORD my God, You are very great: You are clothed with honor and majesty, who cover Yourself with light as with a garment, who stretch out the heavens like a curtain.*

> PSALM 104:1-2

Can you imagine what it is going to be like in heaven with the brilliance of Jesus Christ sitting on His throne with an innumerable host of worshiping angels declaring, "Lord God Almighty"?

Is the light of the Gospel message shining in your hearts today? The Apostle John has declared this message to us:

> *This is the message which we have heard from Him and declare to you, that God is light and in Him is no darkness at all.*

> 1 JOHN 1:5

3

THE STANDARD OF PERFECTION

MATTHEW 5:17-22

In setting the background for this next chapter, Jesus finished teaching His disciples the incredible Beatitudes. He set forth the disciples' characteristics, influence and responsibilities in the kingdom of God. Remember, Jesus was speaking to His disciples, Christians like us—the Church—not to the world, as they would not understand these precepts.

THE LAW FULFILLED — Matthew 5:17-18

"Do not think that I [Jesus] came to destroy the Law or the Prophets. I did not come to destroy but to fulfill. For assuredly, I say to you, till heaven and earth pass away, one jot or one tittle will by no means pass from the law till all is fulfilled."

Jesus began teaching the Beatitudes with being *poor in spirit* and ended with instruction on being *salt* and *light*. His disciples needed to let their light shine as they performed good works to the glory of their Father in heaven.

Then Jesus, with authority, declared that He had come to fulfill the Law. He began to explain to His followers His own relationship to the Law of Moses—the first five books of the Old Testament. Jesus did not come to speak about the Law, or even break the Law, but to fulfill it. To *fulfill* means "to make complete or make full." Jesus Christ placed

Himself in that exact meaning. It was His office to fulfill the Law and to bring it to a perfect completeness—fully finished.

Jesus declared to those listening, *"I have come to fulfill the Law and the Prophets,"* the entire Hebrew Scriptures—the Old Testament, "and now I AM here." He viewed His role as the fulfillment of the Old Testament books and its prophecies. Therefore, He did not come to destroy the Law, but to fulfill it in the Spirit, which is much nobler than to fulfill it in the Letter of the Law. Jesus did not come to relax or restrain the Law or destroy its authority. He came to complete it.

Christ also came to do what the Law failed to do. It could not make men righteous. Jesus Christ fulfilled the Law when He abolished our sins on the Cross. He reconciled us to God, making us righteous before Him:

> *Now all things are of God, who has reconciled us to Himself through Jesus Christ.... For He made Him who knew no sin to be sin for us, that we might become the righteousness of God in Him.*

> 2 CORINTHIANS 5:18, 21

No one could ever keep the Law, because of the weakness of men's sinful flesh. Man was so thoroughly lost, Jesus came to pay the penalty for his sins when He died for the sins of mankind, and rose again to give man new life. On the Day of Pentecost, the Holy Spirit came upon His disciples as they gathered to pray in an upper room to empower them to live a holy life (Acts 2). Otherwise, man would still be bound by the requirements of the Law. God loved us so much that He sent His Only Begotten Son, so that we, by faith in Jesus Christ, could be saved:

> *For the law of the Spirit of life in Christ Jesus has made me free from the law of sin and death. For what the law could not do in that it was weak through the flesh, God did by sending His own Son in the likeness of sinful flesh, on account of sin: He condemned sin in the flesh, that the righteous requirement of the law might be fulfilled in us who do not walk according to the flesh but according to the Spirit.*

> ROMANS 8:2-4

If we walk in the power of the Holy Spirit, we are no longer under the Law. If we walk in the flesh, we shall be judged! Seriously, as a Christian, we should have our shoes off and our faces bowed down to the floor because of all that Jesus Christ has done for each of us, individually.

The Representative of the whole human race is traced back to one Man—Jesus Christ. It is important to fully understand why God sent His Only Begotten Son into the world. He is the key to our salvation: *For there is one God and one Mediator between God and men, the Man Christ Jesus, who gave Himself a ransom for all...*(1Timothy 2:5-6). Do not get confused about the way to your salvation. It is by faith in Jesus Christ—period.

Every Jot and Tittle

Whenever Jesus used the phrase, *"For assuredly, I say to you,"* it was imperative for those listening to pay close attention. Jesus was about to say something very important. In this case, it was essential for His disciples to know that He had come, not to destroy the Law, but to fulfill the Law and the Prophets.

Again, the *Law and the Prophets* refers to the entire Old Testament, the Hebrew Scriptures. Not one word would pass from the Law until all was fulfilled—not one *jot*, which is the smallest stroke of a Hebrew letter, or one *tittle*, which is a vowel point the size of a period next to a single Hebrew letter (Matthew 5:18). Jesus proclaimed that everything prophetically written about Him in the Scriptures concerning His First and Second Coming would be fulfilled by Him—amazing!

When a lawyer came to Jesus to test Him, he asked, *"Teacher, which is the great commandment in the law?"* (Matthew 22:36) The lawyer purposely took Jesus back to Deuteronomy 6:4-5. This passage of Scripture is known to Jews as the *Shema,* a prayer taken from the written Law that gives affirmation of God's singularity: *"Hear, O Israel: The LORD our God, the LORD is one! You shall love the LORD your God with all your heart, with all your soul, and with all your strength."*

In response to the lawyer's question, Jesus said:

> " 'You shall love the Lord your God with all your heart, with all your soul, and with all your mind.' This is the first and great commandment. And the second is like it: 'You shall love your neighbor as yourself.' On these two commandments hang all the Law and the Prophets.' "

> MATTHEW 22:37-40

Certainly the first and great commandment was the most important one, but notice, Jesus gave only two commandments to the lawyer, because within these two commandments hangs the entire Law! Jesus gave an amazing statement and a new understanding of a person's relationship with God, in relation to the Law. Jesus contrasted the Old Testament—the Old Covenant with the New Testament—the New Covenant.

The Apostle Paul established what Jesus taught:

> Owe no one anything except to love one another, for he who loves another has fulfilled the law. For the commandments, "You shall not commit adultery," "You shall not murder," "You shall not steal," "You shall not bear false witness," "You shall not covet," and if there is any other commandment, are all summed up in this saying, namely, "You shall love your neighbor as yourself." Love does no harm to a neighbor; therefore love is the fulfillment of the law.

> ROMANS 13:8-10

Christians are to love God and love their neighbor! Sometimes it is hard to love our neighbors, but this is exactly what we are called to do. As believers, we obey the Word of God because of our deep love for Christ, not because we are trying to make ourselves righteous by it. That would be impossible.

What Is the Purpose of the Law?

In giving the Law to Moses, God has revealed to mankind His holiness. His character is holy: " '...*for I the* LORD *am holy...*' " (Leviticus 20:26), and the Law of God is holy:...*the law is holy, and the commandment holy and just and good* (Romans 7:12).

We have all broken God's Law and miserably fail to keep His Ten Commandments, so the Law points to our sinfulness: *Therefore by the deeds of the law no flesh will be justified in His sight, for by the law is the knowledge of sin* (Romans 3:20). The Law shows us that we are all guilty before a holy God—it condemns us:

> *What shall we say then? Is the law sin? Certainly not! On the contrary, I would not have known sin except through the law. For I would not have known covetousness unless the law had said, "You shall not covet."*

> ROMANS 7:7

You see, even though the Law reveals our sin, it also acts as a guardian, a tutor to point us to the Cross—it leads us to Christ:

> *Therefore the law was our tutor to bring us to Christ, that we might be justified by faith. But after faith has come, we are no longer under a tutor. For you are all sons of God through faith in Christ Jesus.*

> GALATIANS 3:24-26

So the Law of God brings us to conviction, to our knees—to Jesus Christ. It is only when we accept Christ as our Savior that He forgives us and washes away our sins. A repentant sinner receives God's grace— His unmerited favor. Believers in Christ now live their lives under the grace of God. Charles Spurgeon believed that people "will never accept grace until they tremble before a just and holy law." I like that.

Dwight L. Moody was born on February 5, 1837. He earned a living selling shoes in his uncle's store in Boston. As a teenager, he attended Sunday school and became a Christian at the age of 18. Soon after that, Moody moved to Chicago, where he was determined to make his fortune selling shoes.

Instead, in the slums of Chicago, God placed a call on his life to reach the poor. From that time forward, he lived a well-lived life for Christ. He began a church (from which, six years later, was formed the Illinois Street Independent Church, a foundation to the now famous Moody Memorial Church). As a preacher of the kingdom of God, he simply summed up Law and grace this way: "The Law tells me how crooked I am. Grace comes along to straighten me out."

Christians no longer have to live in bondage to the Law; their lives are lived under God's unmerited favor—God's grace. God has given us a free will. We can choose to obey by faith the Word of God, so that when we die, we no longer fear death and hell. We are forgiven, and heaven awaits us. That is what the Bible teaches. It is such good news!

Yet there are people who are still, in futility, trying to fulfill the Law by doing works. Talk to these religious people, and they will argue with you and revile you. There is absolutely no conviction in their lives. The same problem existed with the Pharisees, Sadducees and scribes. They had conformity to the Law, a lot of religion and tradition, but no real spiritual conviction.

The scribes and Pharisees were believed to be guardians of the Law. Yet Jesus would expose these religious leaders' hypocrisy to the Law. They hated Jesus and could not stand Him because they only had religion, no genuine relationship with God that comes through faith in Jesus Christ.

In fact, the Jewish leaders were very proud of their heritage. They traced their ancestry back to their Fathers—Abraham, Isaac, Jacob and Moses—back to the constitution of God, the foundation of their nation. Yet when you trace the nation of Israel's history back to when they were delivered out of Egypt, many of the people murmured, complained and rebelled against God in the wilderness (Exodus 15:24; Exodus 16-17).

In Exodus 21-23, God gave Moses various Laws; and in Exodus 24:7, we find these entire sections were compiled together in what is known as the Book of the Covenant. Moses read to the people from this Book, and after hearing these judgments of God, the children of Israel said with one voice:

> *"...All that the LORD has said we will do, and be obedient." And Moses took the blood, sprinkled it on the people, and said, "This is the blood of the covenant which the LORD has made with you according to all these words."*

EXODUS 24:7-8

After giving further instructions, God called Moses up to Mount Sinai to receive the two Tablets of Testimony, also known as the Ten Commandments written with the finger of God on tablets of stone (Exodus 31:18). As Moses delayed, in his absence, the people built a golden calf to worship! When Moses eventually came down from the mountain, at the sight of Israel's idolatry, he threw down the stone tablets and they broke (Exodus 32:19).

Moses commanded a separation be made, that those who were on God's side come to him, so the sons of Levi gathered to Moses. At his command, in judgment, about three thousand people were ordered killed by God (Exodus 32:26-28). God again called Moses back to Mount Sinai. He remained there for forty days and forty nights, and during that time, he again received *the words of the covenant, the Ten Commandments* written on tablets of stone (Exodus 34:28).

Sadly, throughout the Old Testament, God's people continually failed to keep the Law. The Jewish leaders who addressed Christ tried to go back to this Covenant as their proud, ancestral foundation.

Consequently, Jesus declared, "I Am the fulfillment of the Law! I Am the Constitution of God!"

UNDERSTANDING THE LAW — Matthew 5:19

> "Whoever therefore breaks one of the least of these commandments, and teaches men so, shall be called least in the kingdom of heaven; but whoever does and teaches them, he shall be called great in the kingdom of heaven."

Since every *jot* and *tittle* of the Law remains in force, undiminished, it is a sin to violate or to break even the least of the Commandments or to teach others to do so. Jesus' reference to *one of the least of these commandments* shows that the Jews were in the habit of classifying various commandments. The sin of stealing was not as bad as murder. It does not work that way. Sin is sin.

The word *break* is translated "to destroy." It is used in regards to the Law, in acting contrary to the Law. In the English language, we simply speak of "breaking the law." The word *break* can also mean "to lose or to pull down," by teaching error concerning the Law and by not teaching the truth. So to teach that Jesus destroyed the Law or did away with it would be to teach error. Jesus did not get rid of the Law, the Ten Commandments; He fulfilled it!

The Apostle James understood and plainly pointed out this truth: *For whoever shall keep the whole law, and yet stumble in one point, he is guilty of all* (James 2:10). The Law in its entirety! That is why both Jews and Gentiles are pointed toward the Cross where Christ died for the sins of the world. Everyone has an opportunity to access salvation by faith in Him.

The Moral, Judicial and Ceremonial Law

The Law consists of the first five books of the Bible—the five books of Moses: Genesis, Exodus, Leviticus, Numbers and Deuteronomy—the remaining 34 books of the Hebrew Scriptures are known as the Prophets. Both the Law and the Prophets together gave the standard for Jewish living. Now the Bible is comprised of a further 27 books of the New Testament.

The Law is broken down into three main areas: the Moral Law, the Judicial Law and the Ceremonial Law. What is the Moral Law? The Moral Law is written in Exodus 20:1-17, and it addresses people's moral behavior. These Ten Commandments were given to Moses, but later, in addition to them, the Pharisees added another 613 laws which brought God's people into bondage.

The Judicial Law deals with penalties and judgments written in the books of Exodus, Leviticus, Numbers and Deuteronomy. The Ceremonial Law relates to the offerings, such as the peace offerings, the sin offerings, the burnt sacrifices offered to God, as well as Israel's observances of the feast days, and dietary laws.

Within all these sacrifices and offerings are types, pictures and shadows of Jesus Christ, which can be found in the New Testament. The sacrifices also point to the consecration of our lives, and the peace offerings are a picture of the sweet fellowship that we can have with Christ. All the way through the Old Testament Scriptures, the Law of God is seen, right up to the book of Malachi which finishes with a curse because no human can fulfill the Law. Yet how does the New Testament begin? It begins with grace.

Can you imagine living during the Old Testament times? If you broke any one of these many Laws, you would have had to make an animal sacrifice. Now in the New Testament, if you sin, you can go directly to Jesus Christ—the Lamb of God who offered Himself as a sacrifice for man's sin. He is our High Priest—who sympathizes with our weaknesses. Therefore, we can come boldly to the throne of grace, that we might obtain mercy and find help in time of need (Hebrews 4:14-16).

Jesus became our sacrifice for sin on the Cross, once and for all:

> And every priest stands ministering daily and offering repeatedly the same sacrifices, which can never take away sins. But this Man, after He had offered one sacrifice for sins forever, sat down at the right hand of God, from that time waiting till His enemies are made His footstool. For by one offering He has perfected forever those [believers] who are being sanctified.
>
> HEBREWS 10:11-14

If anyone sins after they have been forgiven through Jesus Christ's sacrifice on the Cross, they have an Advocate with the Father:

> My little children, these things I write to you, so that you may not sin. And if anyone sins, we have an Advocate with the Father, Jesus Christ the righteous. And He Himself is the propitiation [sin offering, appeasing, atonement] for our sins, and not for ours only but also for the whole world.
>
> 1 JOHN 2:1-2

Amazing—Amazing!

IMPOSSIBLE PERFECTION — Matthew 5:20

> "For I say to you, that unless your righteousness exceeds the righteousness of the scribes and Pharisees, you will by no means enter the kingdom of heaven."

Jesus turned His attention to the person who discovers and appropriates the truth of righteousness and manifests the character and qualities that are described in the Beatitudes (Matthew 5:3-12). I love this! In other words, Jesus made it plainly understood that no one can be saved by their own righteousness. It is an impossible perfection.

What did Jesus mean when He spoke about righteousness? The Pharisees, Sadducees and scribes were very self-righteous. They trusted in their own righteousness and believed they could be saved by the Law. Not so! Jesus repudiated these pious guardians of the Law. Their self-righteousness was an unreachable pinnacle of hypocrisy. All their religious works were done in pride—it was all for nothing.

When the Pharisees, Sadducees and scribes openly prayed in the streets and piously fasted, it was to be seen by men (Matthew 6:2, 5, 16). They would roll out a mat to pray, saying, "Lord, I thank you so much that I am not a Gentile." You see, the Pharisees despised others. They thought they were so much more righteous than anyone else.

The Pharisees were very self-righteous when giving their offerings. Everything they did was to be seen by men; they loved to be thought of as holy (Matthew 23:5). In contrast, Jesus drew His disciples' attention to a poor widow who humbly gave her offering to the Lord. He said of her,

> *"Truly I say to you that this poor widow has put in more than all; for all these out of their abundance have put in offerings for God, but she out of her poverty put in all the livelihood that she had"* (Luke 21:3-4).

The Law was not given to Abraham; it was given to Moses. Even though Abraham was not under the Law, if you follow the footsteps of his life, he lived by faith in God's promises, without even having the Law. It was his faith that accounted him righteous (Genesis 17:10-14; Romans 4:9-12; Hebrews 11:8-12).

This brings up a very good point. When we are born into this world, and as we grow and mature, instinctively we become aware of what is right and wrong. Even if we have no biblical knowledge of the Scriptures, our conscience knows the difference between sin and righteousness. Ultimately, man searches for God and can find Him: *Then you will call upon Me and go and pray to Me, and I will listen to you. And you will seek Me and find Me, when you search for Me with all your heart* (Jeremiah 29:12-13).

Man's Religious Traditions

The religious elites questioned Jesus about His disciples, asking, *"Why do Your disciples transgress the tradition of the elders? For they do not wash their hands when they eat bread."* What did Jesus answer them?

> *"Why do you also transgress the commandment of God because of your tradition? For God commanded, saying, 'Honor your father and your mother'; and, 'He who curses father or mother, let him be put to death.' But you say, 'Whoever says to his father or mother, "Whatever profit you might have received from me is a gift to God"—then he need not honor his father or mother.' Thus you have made the commandment of God of no effect by your tradition. Hypocrites! Well did Isaiah prophesy about you, saying: 'These people draw near to Me with their mouth, and honor Me with their lips, but their heart is far from Me. And in vain they worship Me, teaching as doctrines the commandments of men.'"*

MATTHEW 15:3-9

Tradition! Tradition! Tradition! Jesus' piercing words left them to think. Again, they needed to have faith in Christ, but all they had was vain works and empty traditions.

Therefore, Jesus gave a serious warning to those who would try to attain righteousness before God by their own self-righteousness: *"... you will by no means enter the kingdom of heaven"* (Matthew 5:20). Those listening needed to understand that only true faith in Christ saves them.

The Pharisees, Sadducees and scribes had missed the point of Jesus' coming. He came to save mankind through His righteousness: *For He [God] made Him [Jesus] who knew no sin to be sin for us,* [taking our sins on Himself, to the Cross] *that we might become the righteousness of God in Him* (2 Corinthians 5:21).

The Tradition of Attending Church

All around the world, people from all walks of life will traditionally attend church services. Why do people go to church? Attending church can be for various reasons. Maybe a person goes because of guilt or a sense of duty. Others may be trying to please a spouse or other family members. I believe with all my heart, many people feel good about themselves when they go to church.

Then, of course, there are those who attend church for the right reasons. They want to learn the Word of God, and they have a real desire to know God. In sincerity, they seek Him so they can have a change of heart and live a life for Christ. Charles Spurgeon also had thoughts on the reasons why people come to church. Consider his comments:

> "Some go to church to take a walk; some go there to laugh and talk. Some go there to meet a friend; some go there their time to spend. Some go there to meet a lover; some go there a fault to cover. Some go there for speculation; some go there for observation. Some go there to doze and nod; the wise go there to worship God."

Many people who attend church are hoping to be saved by their own righteousness, but they cannot. Our righteousness is as filthy rags (Isaiah 64:6). A self-righteous person may think they are a good enough person to enter heaven, yet in truth, there will be a lot of good people in hell who rejected Christ, who will be separated from God for all eternity!

Understand, it is not about you and me—it is about Jesus Christ. Do not be as the self-righteous Pharisees, having your own flawed righteousness. Salvation is only by faith in Jesus Christ. When we humble ourselves and, by faith, accept Jesus as Savior, we become righteous. He is our Righteousness.

Christians live by faith. *Now faith is the substance* [assurance] *of things hoped for, the evidence* [reality] *of things not seen* (Hebrews 11:1). As it is written in the Word of God, *"The just shall live by faith"* (Romans 1:17). We walk by faith: *For we walk by faith, not by sight* (2 Corinthians 5:7). Believers are to pray by faith (Matthew 6:6) and resist evil by faith: *...above all, taking the shield of faith with which you will be able to quench all the fiery darts of the wicked one* (Ephesians 6:16).

Christians overcome by faith: *For whatever is born of God overcomes the world. And this is the victory that has overcome the world—our faith* (1 John 5:4). Then finally, a believer in Christ dies by faith: *These all died in faith, not having received the promises, but having seen them afar off were assured of them, embraced them and confessed that they were strangers and pilgrims on the earth* (Hebrews 11:13).

We are pilgrims on earth, this is not our home. Our home is heaven. There is only one way we are going to get there—faith in Jesus Christ. There is an appointed time for a person to die. When a child of God dies, they are carried by the angels into the holy presence of God.

IN DANGER OF JUDGMENT — Matthew 5:21-22

> "You have heard that it was said to those of old, 'You shall not murder, and whoever murders will be in danger of the judgment.' But I say to you that whoever is angry with his brother without a cause shall be in danger of the judgment. And whoever says to his brother, 'Raca!' shall be in danger of the council. But whoever says, 'You fool!' shall be in danger of hell fire."

When Jesus made reference to *those of old*, He was speaking of the ancients—the teachers of the Old Testament. Jesus quoted the sixth Commandment, *"You shall not murder"* (Exodus 20:13). If a person murdered someone, then according to the Law, they would pay with their own life for another man's blood—life for life.

God established capital punishment for those who committed murder, in the time of Noah, before the Law was given: *"Whoever sheds man's blood, by man his blood shall be shed; for in the image of God He made man"* (Genesis 9:6). Jewish courts acted in compliance to the Law as recorded in Exodus 21:12: *"He who strikes a man so that he dies shall surely be put to death."* and in Leviticus 24:17: *"Whoever kills any man shall surely be put to death."* The perpetrator was to be stoned to death.

Jesus declared what the Law said, but He took it a step further: *But I say to you that whoever is angry with his brother without a cause shall be in danger of the judgment.* Even though a person may not commit the physical act of murder, they, through anger, could commit murder inwardly in their heart.

Jesus gave this contrast to draw people to understand rightly the Law of God. A person could simply be angry with their brother and still be found guilty of murder and face God's judgment. It is God who searches men's heart (Jeremiah 17:9), and it is from the heart that man sins:

> *"...those things which proceed out of the mouth come from the heart, and they defile a man. For out of the heart proceed evil thoughts, murders, adulteries, fornications, thefts, false witness, blasphemies. These are the things which defile a man...."*
>
> MATTHEW 15:18-20

Murder is born from within the heart from an uncontrolled spirit and an unregulated urge from an inner anger that has been settled in a person's heart for a long time. Anger is a real sin, and sin breaks the Law of God. This is a difficult lesson because we all have a hard time with anger. Most people get angry just driving on the freeway! Anger is felt in an instant fury, and we know we have to repent before the Lord. Consider the marked difference when someone has held on to anger and resentment for years and years. Anger builds within them until it reaches a boiling point where they feel like they want to kill someone. That is how far anger can take a person!

I believe many Christians have not given any thought about the anger hidden within their hearts. In our new relationship with Christ, under His grace, if a relationship is broken with a brother in Christ because of anger, it is not right before Him. In 1 John 4:20 it states: *If someone says, "I love God," and hates his brother, he is a liar; for he who does not love his brother whom he has seen, how can he love God whom he has not seen?*

As a Christian, it is important to discern the conviction of the Holy Spirit. If there is no conviction, then something is absolutely wrong; you are not listening to the voice of God. If you are cold-hearted and do not feel bad about your anger and murderous thoughts, then something is definitely wrong with your relationship with God.

Deny anger! Be slow to anger! In Proverbs 14:17, it tells us: *A quick-tempered man acts foolishly....* Can you relate to that? In Ephesians 4:26-27, it tells us: *"Be angry, and do not sin" : do not let the sun go down on your wrath, nor give place to the devil.* Every day our hearts need to be kept clean before God (Psalm 51:10). Do we truly love people or hate them? Ask God to remove any hateful anger from your heart.

Jesus spoke plainly and understandably in all that He instructed. Christians need to be very careful with the words they speak. The word *Raca* means "empty headed or brainless idiot." The word *fool* means "moron or stupid." This is a big problem with people who constantly offend and demean others. How many of us are guilty of calling people "stupid" or "idiot"? Jesus warned people that those who say such things were in danger of hell fire, which is a place of judgment in Gehenna—the Lake of Fire.

Yet how many parents call their children stupid or dummy? When they are grown, the view of themselves is damaged. They feel stupid, as if they can do nothing right—sad. Children have been greatly hurt by those words. Christians are no longer to demean or embarrass anyone by calling them stupid, especially parents to their children. Instead, they are to build up their children.

Christians can be guilty of offending people with words said in anger. Once spoken, it is too late to take back offensive words said from the heart. Any anger that arises in our hearts needs to be short-lived. When we feel angry, it is better to close our mouths and not say anything; just open the door and go take a walk. We should allow God to speak to our hearts so that when we return home, we can build up others with our words and not tear them down. It is important to understand, God keeps a record of every idle word we say! He can help us to have control of our mouths so we do not sin against Him.

The Law of God pointed out man's sin. When Jesus fulfilled the Law through His coming, He gave us unmerited favor through His sacrificial death on the Cross—abolishing our sins once and for all. His grace will enable us to live the Christian life. Prayerfully, as we continue to learn from Christ's *Sermon of Sermons,* there will be a noticeable change in our lives. We need to fear the Lord—bottom line.

4

FORGIVENESS AND RECONCILIATION

MATTHEW 5:23-26

Jesus taught on a subject that most people struggle with, and, I am sure, they would rather avoid—forgiveness and reconciliation.

A MATTER OF THE HEART — Matthew 5:23-24

"Therefore if you bring your gift to the altar, and there remember that your brother has something against you, leave your gift there before the altar, and go your way. First be reconciled to your brother, and then come and offer your gift."

In Jewish culture as taught in the Old Testament, a person would come to the altar to give their sacrifice to atone for sin. Jesus taught that before a gift was given to God, an examination of the heart was necessary.

If a person remembered that he was the cause of an offense that a brother held against him, then he was to leave his gift at the altar and make things right with the brother. He was to be reconciled to the brother first before his gift was acceptable to God. In this way, he was granted peace in his life.

Again, Jesus dealt with the heart of His disciples, just as He deals with each one of us. When a Christian is sitting in church, before they give their offering, they should listen to the Word of God and take an examination of their heart. If all of a sudden, they remember a brother or sister in Christ who has something against them, they should first make things right with them. They are to be reconciled to their brother or sister in Christ before giving their gift to the Lord.

It is important not to run away from these uncomfortable situations. God will not accept our gifts until we have gone to the person we have offended and made things right with them. Ask people to forgive you for whatever it is you have done toward them. Prayerfully approach them and tell them, "If I have done anything against you, I apologize; I am sorry." Again, once you have made the effort to make things right, leave the situation alone. God knows that you have tried to make things right before Him.

Unforgiveness

After a time of examination of your heart, perhaps you find that you have not hurt anyone else, but someone has hurt you. Is there someone who dislikes or hates you? It is still good to examine your heart and ask the Lord, "Is there anything I have done against them to cause them to hate me?" In doing so, you are making sure nothing is hindering your relationship with God.

Some Christians cannot forgive someone who has hurt them. Yet how can they continue to receive God's forgiveness for themselves if they are unforgiving and have a hardened heart against someone else? Later in Jesus' sermon, He would sternly warn against the sin of unforgiveness: *But if you do not forgive men their trespasses, neither will your Father forgive your trespasses* (Matthew 6:15).

Christians need to forgive. Remember, Jesus bore the punishment for our sins on the Cross. Jesus loves us. He forgave us. If Jesus willingly demonstrated His love and forgiveness toward us, then how much more should we forgive others? Believers in Christ are to sacrificially love people and willingly forgive them for the offenses made against them regardless of their responses.

There are some people who attend church every week, but they leave exactly the same way—unchanged. I believe with all my heart, they have not really taken to heart what the Word of God has taught them. The Scriptures are very clear about forgiveness.

If a Christian harbors any anger or bitterness toward someone who has offended them, they may come to a point of hoping this person would never prosper, or they could secretly wish them dead! These are some of the hidden sins deep within a person's heart that God sees. It reveals the evilness of the human heart. A child of God cannot get away with sin.

Any sin grieves the Holy Spirit of God who dwells within us:....*do not grieve the Holy Spirit of God, by whom you were sealed for the day of redemption* (Ephesians 4:30). The word *grieve* in the Greek means "bring pain." The Holy Spirit is a Person; He can be hurt. Honestly, the only answer to bitterness and anger harbored in a person's heart is unconditional forgiveness—period:

> *Let all bitterness, wrath, anger, clamor, and evil speaking be put away from you, with all malice. And be kind to one another, tenderhearted, forgiving one another, even as God in Christ forgave you.*

> EPHESIANS 4:31-32

As a Christian, you cannot harbor hatred, bitterness or anger in your heart toward someone else. If you want to be free in Christ, for God to speak to your heart, and for the Lord to use your life, then make things right with whoever has offended you or whoever you have offended. To the best of your ability, try to reconcile with them. Ask God to help you resolve these issues quickly; do not let them fester—real important!

Forgiveness Within Families

Unforgiveness exists within families. It is possible for you to hold on to feelings of anger, bitterness and hatred toward a family member for years. Then again, it can be just as probable for a family member to hold these same feelings against you.

If you have done anything to offend a person in your family, then try to make it right. If they choose not to forgive you, then at least you have tried your best. Leave the situation in the hands of God, knowing that you were obedient to Him. God will now accept your gift, just as Jesus taught in Matthew 5:23-24, and your fellowship with Him will remain unhindered.

Know this: when families separate because of harsh words said in anger, it becomes a bad witness to their children. The offense, coupled with unforgiveness, causes families to divide. Sadly, cousins can become separated from their other cousins. That is not right. Imagine, these children want to grow up together and love each other, but now they cannot—it is so sad.

When families become angry and oppose each other, the children often get poisoned by their parents. They can grow up hating each other. According to God, that should never be. Families should never become separated—they should learn to forgive and be reconciled.

The answer to unforgiveness is forgiveness and reconciliation— restoration. Then families can worship God together; otherwise, how is worship possible? Worship is unacceptable to God unless family members resolve their issues between themselves.

What about forgiveness between a husband and wife? This can be a real issue in a marriage. Within the heart of a spouse, they can hold on to anger, bitterness and hatred. A husband and wife can literally live within the same house and yet have no verbal communication or intimate connection.

This is well known among couples as giving each other the silent treatment. Spouses refuse to respond to each other. This neglect to communicate will destroy their marriage. Why is it that so many spouses find it so hard to say they are sorry? I believe it is often pride that stands in the way. The couple has built solid walls between themselves that will need to be broken down.

Reconciliation is necessary. This is accomplished through humility, open communication, love and forgiveness. For those husbands struggling in their marriages, listen to the Apostle Paul. He instructs: *Husbands, love your wives and do not be bitter toward them* (Colossians 3:19). Husbands love your wives! Husbands are to be the spiritual leaders of the home. Can you obediently apply this verse to your marriage? Can you forgive your wife? Think about it. Your sons and daughters are watching you. One day they are going to have a family, and they will follow the example you have given them. Children and grandchildren need to see love and unity in a marriage.

In the Scriptures, the younger wives were admonished by the older women in Christ *to love their husbands...* (Titus 2:4). Wives, ask the Lord to give you a loving, devoted heart toward your husband. Can you forgive your husband? It is important to continually forgive one another in a marriage. God wants to bless your family!

What about sons and daughters who need to forgive their parents? In obedience to God's Word, humbly take a step of faith toward forgiving them. Let your parents know you forgive them for whatever hurt you held against them, and God will honor you. Make sure your heart is right with God and right with them.

As a child, I grew up watching my mom face tremendous difficulties as she dealt with an alcoholic husband. I hated my mom for the situation. Why did she stay? I gave her a real hard time. When I was saved, one of the first things I did was to go to my mom and dad and ask them both to forgive me for the way I acted toward them—especially my mom. Over the years, they both accepted the Lord and grew in their new found faith. Even though they had divorced, in Christ they decided to remarry. After my father died, and my mother grew frail and old, I used to pick her up every single Sunday so she could attend church. Without fail, after every service, she wanted me to take her to the Wienerschnitzel for a hot dog and, afterward, to the Dairy Queen to eat an ice cream!

Before my mom passed away, I sat quietly with her and gently spoke to her. At this time, she was unable to open her eyes, but she responded to me with her hands. I told her, "I want you again to forgive me for everything I have done to you." I wanted to make sure she understood. She took my hand and squeezed it twice, as if to say, "Do not worry about it—I love you, and I care for you." Then, two days later, she went to be with the Lord. Sometimes, children do not realize how important their mothers are until they are in heaven—how much they did for them, loved and cared for them.

The greatest result of forgiveness is you will have peace in your life and unbroken fellowship with God. You will be able to sleep at night! Imagine the amount of people who cannot even sleep at night because of what they have said or done to their families—so sad. Husbands destroy their wives, and wives destroy their husbands, and parents destroy their children.

Families are splintered as they separate or divorce. Inevitably, the children are devastated. As they grow up in a divided family, they often become hard and bitter against their parents, and end up hating them.

If children, because of a divorce, are alternately living between two homes, then make sure, when they are with you, your actions and words are in their best interests. Do not speak maliciously of another parent in front of them. As much as possible, cooperate with your estranged spouse in schedules and the children's activities. God will take care of the rest, but you have to forgive—forgive—forgive.

Obey what is said in the Word of God so you do not get bitter and poison your children. Ask for your children's forgiveness for the situation, even if you feel it is not your fault. Sometimes it is beneficial to just take the blame. Love your children—love them—love them.

If you have been divorced, do not become condemned. God has forgiven you. If you are remarried, make the best of your marriage—love your husband, love your wife, and make sure you sit down to read the Bible, worship and pray together.

God's Forgiveness and Reconciliation

God's forgiveness and reconciliation—restoration to God are available to every person. Sin has separated us from God: *But your iniquities have separated you from your God; and your sins have hidden His face from you, so that He will not hear* (Isaiah 59:2); but through God's Only Begotten Son, He has given us the way to be reconciled to Him:

> *Now all things are of God, who has reconciled us to Himself through Jesus Christ...that is, that God was in Christ reconciling the world to Himself, not imputing their trespasses to them....*

2 CORINTHIANS 5:18-19

Knowing this truth, just as we have been forgiven of our sins and have made things right with God, the Lord desires for us to forgive others. Later, within the Model Prayer, Jesus would again teach on this: *And forgive us our debts, as we forgive our debtors* (Matthew 6:12). Think about it, is there anyone whom you need to forgive?

The Parable of the Unforgiving Servant

Jesus had twelve disciples, among them was Peter. He came to the Lord and asked a good question: *"Lord, how often shall my brother sin against me, and I forgive him? Up to seven times?"* (Matthew 18:21) Peter was outspoken and very sure of himself. To him, forgiving someone seven times sounded pretty reasonable.

However, Jesus answered Peter, *"I do not say to you, up to seven times, but up to seventy times seven"* (Matthew 18:22). Incredibly, Peter needed to learn to forgive his brother 490 times! Jesus wanted him to understand the concept; in reality, he needed to forgive the offenses of a brother all the time—continuously.

Then Jesus continued to share a parable about forgiveness with all those listening. Again Jesus dealt with the human heart, as most people do not like to forgive. In this case, a certain king wanted to settle accounts with his servants: *"And when he had begun to settle accounts, one was brought to him who owed him ten thousand talents"* (Matthew 18:24). The amount was about $3.48 billion in today's economy! Imagine that! The servant was unable to pay this vast amount, so *"his master commanded that he be sold with his wife and children and all that he had, and that payment be made"* (Matthew 18:25).

If the servant was thrown into prison, how could he expect to clear his debt? He could not! The man, fully aware of his awful predicament, immediately fell down to beg the king, saying, " *'Master, have patience with me, and I will pay you all' "* (Matthew 18:26). The servant promised to pay everything he owed the king if he was released. He would work hard to pay off his debt.

As a result, *"...the master of that servant was moved with compassion, released him, and forgave him his debt"* (Matthew 18:27). His master was merciful and told the troubled servant, "Forget the debt; you owe me nothing." Imagine the weight of his burden released from his shoulders! Yet look what happened next in Matthew 18:28:

> *"But that servant went out and found one of his fellow servants who owed him a hundred denarii* [about $15,000]; *and he laid hands on him and took him by the throat, saying, 'Pay me what you owe!' "*

Can you believe that? Jesus in His parable gave an example of a king who forgave a servant an astronomical amount, yet in return, this same servant pursued a fellow servant who owed him a much smaller amount of money. He used harsh judgment against him:

> *"So his fellow servant fell down at his feet and begged him, saying, 'Have patience with me, and I will pay you all.' And he would not, but went and threw him into prison till he should pay the debt."*

> MATTHEW 18:29-30

When was his fellow servant able to pay? He was thrown in prison—so, never! The unjust servant showed no mercy and no grace, even though he had just been forgiven so much by his master! This truly showed the servant's heart of unforgiveness. In his life, there was no true repentance. Jesus continued, *"So when his fellow servants saw what had been done, they were very grieved, and came and told their master all that had been done"* (Matthew 18:31).

Could you imagine how you would you feel if you had forgiven someone, and you heard they went out and threatened someone like this wicked servant did? You would be pretty mad! Despite the compassion his master had just shown him, the servant lacked pity toward his fellow servant. As a result:

> *"...his master, after he had called him, said to him, 'You wicked servant! I forgave you all that debt because you begged me. Should you not also have had compassion on your fellow servant, just as I had pity on you?' And his master was angry, and delivered him to the torturers until he should pay all that was due to him."*

> MATTHEW 18:32-34

Notice, the servant's master did not mess around—judgment came swiftly. He had given his servant an amazing opportunity—he had forgiven him his debt—so why could this servant not show the same compassion toward his fellow servant and forgive him?

Jesus concluded the parable by addressing all the people who listened: *"So My heavenly Father also will do to you if each of you, from his heart, does not forgive his brother his trespasses"* (Matthew 18:35). Jesus' parable is a warning to each of us! We have been forgiven of all our sins—all our mistakes, everything—so we need to be forgiving toward others. If we truly believe in forgiveness for ourselves, then why is it so hard to forgive others?

As a Christian, you need to forgive your family, friends, and even your enemies; otherwise, how can you expect Jesus to forgive you? How many times are you to forgive? Jesus said 70 x 7= 490 times; in other words, you are to forgive always!

MAKE PEACE QUICKLY — Matthew 5:25-26

"Agree with your adversary quickly, while you are on the way with him, lest your adversary deliver you to the judge, the judge hand you over to the officer, and you be thrown into prison. Assuredly, I say to you, you will by no means get out of there till you have paid the last penny."

In His sermon Jesus exhorted His listeners to agree with their adversary quickly—not next year, quickly! Once again, we learn that those called to follow Jesus must seek to forgive the offenses others have done against them. Believers are not to linger in settling matters with someone who has become their adversary. Reconciliation should be sought out immediately—as soon as they can do it!

Believers in Christ should quickly make peace with anyone who has become an enemy through strife, unforgiveness or disagreements. Ask God for wisdom. Prayerfully, and as peaceably as possible, work toward making things right.

Jesus gave this analogy to His followers to help them understand why they needed to forgive others, *"...agree with your adversary quickly... lest your adversary deliver you to the judge...."* If a person was thrown into prison and unable to get out, how could they pay off a debt to the last penny? They could not pay anything! Once the Judge pronounced judgment, there was no longer any opportunity for them to make things right.

The judgment is sure. They are in prison permanently—forever. This analogy mirrors the horrors of a sinner lost for all eternity. Once separated from God in eternal darkness, there is no escape from Gehenna—the Lake of Fire. A person is there forever and ever.

From this lesson, Christians learn that it is best, while they have the opportunity, to quickly forgive others and restore peace. As the Holy Spirit speaks to your own heart, may He convict you. Be on your knees before God and ask Him, "Is there anything within me that is hindering my fellowship with You? Show me so I can repent and do what is right."

Christians have a duty to try to settle things with someone, then they can let God be the judge between them. Romans 12:18 tells us: *If it is possible, as much as depends on you, live peaceably with all men.*

Therefore, we should love peace, make peace, live at peace, and be at peace with all people. Are you truly doing this today?

5

THE RIGHT ATTITUDE TOWARD SIN

MATTHEW 5:27-32

Jesus' disciples needed to understand that it was necessary for them to have a correct attitude toward sin. It was important to live a life of integrity and to have a heart governed by a godly moral standard.

LUST BEGINS IN THE HEART — Matthew 5:27-28

"You have heard that it was said to those of old, 'You shall not commit adultery.' But I say to you that whoever looks at a woman to lust for her has already committed adultery with her in his heart."

The scribes and Pharisees were regarded as the scholars of the Hebrew language, and, as such, Christ's disciples would have heard them teach the Law. Jesus quoted from the Ten Commandments as taught by the scribes and Pharisees: " 'You shall not commit adultery' " (Exodus 20:14). Adultery was punishable by death. If a man and a woman were found guilty of committing adultery, they were to be stoned to death: *The man who commits adultery with another man's wife, he who commits adultery with his neighbor's wife, the adulterer and the adulteress, shall surely be put to death* (Leviticus 20:10).

In the New Testament, in the case of the adulterous woman, Jesus became her soul's Advocate. He saved her from being stoned to death (John 8:3-11). In the Sermon on the Mount, the right intent of God's command was given by our Master Teacher: *But I [Christ] say to you that whoever looks at a woman to lust for her has already committed adultery with her in his heart"* (Matthew 5:28).

You see, it is not just the physical act of adultery that makes a person an adulterer—adultery begins in the heart. On another occasion, Jesus told His disciples: *"For out of the heart proceed evil thoughts, murders, adulteries, fornications, thefts, false witness, blasphemies"* (Matthew 15:19).

A man or woman can become so obsessed in their heart with wanting someone else's spouse. This uncontrollable, lustful passion can cause them to even lose sleep. They become consumed with thoughts of another person's husband or wife. They crave them as for a forbidden fruit. The desire becomes so strong within them that they will stop at nothing until they get what they want. It is like an irrepressible fever. Lust will drive a person insane!

Often before the physical act of adultery is committed, a person has gone through a thought process. They play with different scenarios within their minds, creating a secret world of lust. When the opportunity arises, adultery is committed. The sin in the heart and mind is acted out. Be careful. Never play with sexual sin in your heart and mind—it will totally destroy you!

Again, if a married man happens to notice a beautiful woman and looks at her once, no problem; but if he looks twice and begins to lust and covet her in his heart, then he has become guilty of adultery before God. Have you heard of the phrase, "The eyes are the windows to the soul"? It is often used in reference to Matthew 6:22-23:

> *"The lamp of the body is the eye. If therefore your eye is good, your whole body will be full of light. But if your eye is bad, your whole body will be full of darkness. If therefore the light that is in you is darkness, how great is that darkness!"*

In the Old Testament, a righteous man named Job made a covenant with his eyes. In Job 31:1, He voiced his unwavering decision not to lust after a woman: *"I have made a covenant with my eyes; why then should I look upon a young woman?"* Why is it that so many believers in the church fail to make the same commitment? We all need to follow Job's example. Why not make a covenant with your eyes before God?

Adultery's Path of Destruction

Adultery destroys marriages. Statistics for 2021 record that there are 750,000 divorces in the U.S. per year. The U.S. divorce rate is among one of the highest in the world. Although divorces in America are on the decline, about 40% to 50% of marriages will still end in divorce. Up to 40% of these divorces are linked to infidelity. It is documented that most people who engage in marital affairs are surprisingly in their 50s or 60s. The divorce rate for people over 50—those who have been married between 20-30 years—has doubled since 1990.

Adultery causes great emotional pain. Those who have suffered the agony of divorce because of adultery have voiced that the trust they once shared and enjoyed in their marriage relationship has now been wrecked. Selfishly, a husband or wife leaves a devastated spouse to remain with the person they have fallen into adultery with—sad.

Marital affairs often begin on the internet. Relationships are easily established in chat rooms and gaming websites.

Adulterous connections are easily made in gyms. You see, most men who like to maintain their bodies by working out at the gym are also looking for and lusting after women—married or single. Many men have inflated egos, and they seem to have a need for attention and interaction. When an immoral man approaches a woman, he easily begins to have a conversation with her. Friendly communication is established, and so is an open door to share about their marital problems. An attraction develops, and pretty soon they are sleeping together. There are married men who will sit with their girlfriends in other churches without conviction and without their wives even knowing! It happens all the time!

Some husbands and wives who commit adultery often carry the heavy weight of guilt because of the sin of adultery. Imagine, in an attempt to hide their sin, they have to play the part of a hypocrite—acting as if everything is fine. Too often their spouse discerns something is not right within their marriage. Once the adulterous affair is uncovered, a devastated spouse may choose not to forgive them, but to divorce. When family and close friends find out, they become angry and upset. Neighbors will gossip and shame is felt. The home becomes divided, children are hurt, and the marriage is destroyed. A jealous husband may seek out the man responsible for committing adultery with his wife. Think about it. An adulterer risks getting killed!

It was the sin of adultery that caused considerable destruction in David's life. It all began when David was idle and not engaged in battle. He came out onto the roof of his house and saw a beautiful woman bathing. David's first look at this attractive woman was not a problem, but it was the second, lingering look that caused him to lust after her. Acting in accordance with his lust, he ordered his servants to bring Bathsheba to his palace. David desired Bathsheba, and his lust led him to commit adultery with her; then afterward she went back home.

A message was sent to David from Bathsheba—she was pregnant! In an attempt to hide his sin, David tried to send her husband Uriah home from battle to sleep with his wife. That failed. So, intentionally, David had Uriah, one of his faithful warriors, killed in battle. David committed murder, and his sin had major consequences. Bathsheba's child died. His immediate family and the entire kingdom of Israel suffered as a result (2 Samuel 11-18). Imagine, David's downfall was a direct result of his adultery. His sin of adultery started with a second, deliberate look at a beautiful woman. From within King David's heart, an evil passion was ignited—sin took hold of him!

Seduced

There are men and women who routinely enjoy the challenge of seducing others. Be careful! Some women will intentionally come to church dressed provocatively. Seductive women have no sense of modesty; they purely seek attention.

A whorish woman will entice single or married men with suggestive language. In Proverbs 6:23-29, we find a strict warning to men about the dangers of being with immoral women:

> *For the commandment is a lamp, and the law a light; reproofs of instruction are the way of life, to keep you from the evil woman, from the flattering tongue of a seductress. Do not lust after her beauty in your heart, nor let her allure you with her eyelids. For by means of a harlot a man is reduced to a crust of bread; and an adulteress will prey upon his precious life. Can a man take fire to his bosom, and his clothes not be burned? Can one walk on hot coals, and his feet not be seared? So is he who goes in to his neighbor's wife; whoever touches her shall not be innocent.*

Despite the warnings about adultery written in the Word of God, there are still so many adulterers in churches. What is the cause of such uncontrolled lust in people's minds? I believe with all my heart, lust is fed by looking at filthy magazines and visiting online pornography sites. Both men and women can get easily get hooked on these vices. Pornography leads to bondage, and ultimately it affects their marriages—period.

Lust is the controlling factor in both the young and the old when they drive the streets looking to hustle a prostitute!

Think about it. They are putting their lives in danger of contracting a venereal disease and taking it home to their spouse. So many people's lives have been ruined physically, emotionally and spiritually by lust—sad.

In fact, when these persons are caught and arrested by undercover police, and arrested, it has even been discovered that some of the perpetrators were actually leaders, and pastors in churches! This is why the Church has no power. Christian leaders live their lives without the fear of God or holiness!

King Solomon, in Proverbs 5:15-20, wisely warned about the idiocies of adultery, and he greatly encouraged a husband's renewed love toward the woman he married:

> *Drink water from your own cistern, and running water from your own well. Should your fountains be dispersed abroad, streams of water in the streets? Let them be only your own, and not for strangers with you. Let your fountain be blessed, and rejoice with the wife of your youth. As a loving deer and a graceful doe, let her breasts satisfy you at all times; and always be enraptured with her love. For why should you, my son, be enraptured by an immoral woman, and be embraced in the arms of a seductress?*

As a Christian, are you willfully committing adultery? May the Holy Spirit bring you to conviction and repentance! God's Word condemns adultery!

CUTTING OFF SIN — Matthew 5:29-30

> "If your right eye causes you to sin, pluck it out and cast it from you; for it is more profitable for you that one of your members perish, than for your whole body to be cast into hell. And if your right hand causes you to sin, cut it off and cast it from you; for it is more profitable for you that one of your members perish, than for your whole body to be cast into hell."

Jesus used this vivid analogy to warn of the dreadful consequences of the sin of adultery. How many times did Jesus refer to the penalties of hell? Twice! It would be far more profitable for a person to enter heaven without a right eye or a right hand than to have their whole body cast into hell. Of course, Jesus did not mean for a person to literally pluck out their eye, as that would not stop them from lusting. Seriously, they would still have a problem with adultery in their mind!

Literally, the word *pluck* means "to take, tear or root out." Jesus warned those listening to His sermon to get rid of sin—cut it off—or sin would destroy them! Sin has to be dealt with because it has deadly consequences. Ridding yourself of sin is accomplished through repentance. Repent of your sin!

Think about it. If a person develops gangrene in an extremity of the body, they cannot allow the infection to spread. Gangrene is not curable. It has to be cut off; otherwise, the rest of the body will become infected. The infection would poison the rest of the body, causing septic shock and resulting in sudden death. It is the same with sin; it needs to be stopped—cut off.

God's Word is very straightforward. The result of adultery, or any other sin, will cause people to perish in eternal fire:

> *Do you not know that the unrighteous will not inherit the kingdom of God? Do not be deceived. Neither fornicators, nor idolaters, nor adulterers, nor homosexuals, nor sodomites, nor thieves, nor covetous, nor drunkards, nor revilers, nor extortioners will inherit the kingdom of God.*

> 1 CORINTHIANS 6:9-10

Those willfully committing adultery would do well to heed the warning found in Galatians 5:19-21:

> *Now the works of the flesh are evident, which are: adultery, fornication, uncleanness, lewdness, idolatry, sorcery, hatred, contentions, jealousies, outbursts of wrath, selfish ambitions, dissensions, heresies, envy, murders, drunkenness, revelries, and*

the like; of which I tell you beforehand, just as I also told you in time past, that those who practice such things will not inherit the kingdom of God.

Adultery is not right before God. He condemns it. Again, where is the conviction of the Holy Spirit and the fear of the Lord? The only way out of an adulterous affair is to repent and bring these sinful passions into submission. Keep your eyes on the Cross, knowing that obedience to God's Word will help you to crucify your flesh and overcome your sinful nature: *And those who are Christ's have crucified the flesh with its passions and desires* (Galatians 5:24).

Are you willing to put a stop to your adultery and cut off the relationship? Will you continue to allow the sin of adultery to destroy your life? Consider this: your decisions have eternal consequences— eternal life or eternal death. Dwight Moody's comment will help you to determine your true spiritual attitude: "Everyone wants to enjoy heaven after they die, but they don't want to be heavenly-minded while they live."

What will you choose to do? The best decision is to repent and tell the person you are committing adultery with that you are done with committing sin.

MARRIAGE AND DIVORCE — Matthew 5:31-32

> "Furthermore it has been said, 'Whoever divorces his wife, let him give her a certificate of divorce.' But I say to you that whoever divorces his wife for any reason except sexual immorality causes her to commit adultery; and whoever marries a woman who is divorced commits adultery."

Jesus addressed another common issue—marriage and divorce. In the Old Testament, in Deuteronomy 24, Laws were established in regards to divorce. Moses had created a document for divorce. Yet husbands were trying to divorce their wives for any simple reason. It could be that a wife placed too much salt in the food, or a husband did not like the way his wife cleaned the house.

When the Pharisees asked Jesus about marriage and divorce, it was only to test Him. They asked Jesus: *"Is it lawful for a man to divorce his wife for just any reason?"* Jesus replied:

> *"Have you not read that He who made them at the beginning 'made them male and female,' and said, 'For this reason a man shall leave his father and mother and be joined to his wife, and the two shall become one flesh'? So then, they are no longer two but one flesh. Therefore what God has joined together, let not man separate."*

> MATTHEW 19:4-6

The Pharisees continued to question Him: *"Why then did Moses command to give a certificate of divorce, and to put her away?"* Jesus replied: *"Moses, because of the hardness of your hearts, permitted you to divorce your wives, but from the beginning it was not so"* (Matthew 19:7-8). Jesus revealed the true reason for why men divorced their wives. It was because of the hardness of man's heart. God, from the beginning, never intended for a man and woman to divorce.

Marriage was instituted in the book of Genesis—right from the beginning of creation. God saw the heart of man, his emptiness and loneliness, so He made a helper for him. God brought the woman to man. Then God blessed the union between one man and one woman:

> *And the LORD God said, "It is not good that man should be alone; I will make him a helper comparable to him." Out of the ground the LORD God formed every beast of the field and every bird of the air, and brought them to Adam to see what he would call them. And whatever Adam called each living creature, that was its name. So Adam gave names to all cattle, to the birds of the air, and to every beast of the field. But for Adam there was not found a helper comparable to him. And the LORD God caused a deep sleep to fall on Adam, and he slept; and He took one of his*

ribs, and closed up the flesh in its place. Then the rib which the LORD God had taken from man He made into a woman, and He brought her to the man.

GENESIS 2:18-22

God established a holy union between one man and one woman before the Law was ever given. Marriage is sacred. Knowing this, Jesus said: *"Therefore what God has joined together, let not man separate"* (Mark 10:9).

Martin Luther was born on November 10, 1483. He became a German theologian and religious reformer who brought about the sixteenth-century Protestant Reformation. Luther commented on the depth of such a holy marriage union: "...there is no more lovely, friendly or charming relationship, communion or company, than a good marriage."

Sadly, married couples think nothing of breaking their sacred vows. They divorce for any apparent reason. Older men will oftentimes leave their wives for younger women! Marriage vows spoken before God must be honored—until death do us part! God hates divorce:

"For the LORD God of Israel says that He hates divorce, for it covers one's garment with violence," says the LORD of hosts. "Therefore take heed to your spirit, that you do not deal treacherously."

MALACHI 2:16

Restoration of a marriage, not its destruction, is always God's goal. The blessings that a marriage can bring should not be cast aside. The Apostle Paul encourages married couples to remain together:

Now to the married I command, yet not I but the Lord: A wife is not to depart from her husband. But even if she does depart, let her remain unmarried or be reconciled to her husband. And a husband is not to divorce his wife. But to the rest I, not the Lord, say: If any brother has a wife who does not believe, and she is

74

willing to live with him, let him not divorce her. And a woman who has a husband who does not believe, if he is willing to live with her, let her not divorce him. For the unbelieving husband is sanctified by the wife, and the unbelieving wife is sanctified by the husband; otherwise your children would be unclean, but now they are holy. But if the unbeliever departs, let him depart; a brother or a sister is not under bondage in such cases. But God has called us to peace. For how do you know, O wife, whether you will save your husband? Or how do you know, O husband, whether you will save your wife?

1 CORINTHIANS 7:10-16

If you accepted the Lord after a divorce and had remarried—all things became brand new: *Therefore, if anyone is in Christ, he is a new creation; old things have passed away; behold, all things have become new* (2 Corinthians 5:17). As you walk with God, remain faithful to the person you have married.

If your spouse dies, as a Christian you can marry again, but only in the Lord:

For the woman who has a husband is bound by the law to her husband as long as he lives. But if the husband dies, she is released from the law of her husband. So then if, while her husband lives, she marries another man, she will be called an adulteress; but if her husband dies, she is free from that law, so that she is no adulteress, though she has married another man.

ROMANS 7:2-3

The Reason for Divorce

Many people ask if there is a legitimate reason for getting a divorce. The Scriptures tell us that God hates divorce (Malachi 2:16). Jesus gave the only reason for divorce—it was for sexual immorality, not for just any cause.

In our society, there are many people who are living lives of adultery. Again, Jesus taught that if a person divorces and remarries for any reason other than sexual immorality (which includes pornography), then in the eyes of God, they are now living in adultery:

> *"...I* [Jesus] *say to you that whoever divorces his wife for any reason except sexual immorality causes her to commit adultery; and whoever marries a woman who is divorced commits adultery."*

MATTHEW 5:32

Living in adultery is not the unpardonable sin, but in the Scriptures, Jesus set a serious precedence of keeping our marriage vows. There needs to be a renewed fear of God in people's lives. Again, before God, the marriage union is sacred.

If adultery is committed, a spouse can divorce, and they are free to marry in the Lord. However, consider what God has said in His Word before acting hastily to divorce your husband or wife. Keep in mind that even if there has been adultery, a wife or husband can choose to forgive their spouse and remain married. Never take actions based on your emotions or your fleshly desires. Give God time to work. Pray for God to give you a renewed love for your spouse. There is a mutual responsibility between husband and wife to fight for their marriage with prayer and fasting (1 Corinthians 7:5).

In difficult situations, such as physical and emotional abuse, drug abuse, and alcohol abuse, first there should be a time of separation to allow God to work in the life of each spouse. A husband and wife will need time to wait upon God to see if there has been a true repentance and change. If there is no change, the marriage can lead to divorce. The Word of God condemns any unrighteousness. God's plan for marriage did not intend for a husband, wife or their children to be destroyed through the abuse of sinful living.

Abstinence

...It is good for a man not to touch a woman. Nevertheless, because of sexual immorality, let each man have his own wife, and let each woman have her own husband.

1 CORINTHIANS 7:1-2

In the Sermon on the Mount, Jesus taught His listeners about the sanctity of marriage (Matthew 5:31-32). The Apostle Paul also taught believers by giving them marriage guidelines. He first addressed those who were single. They should abstain from sexual relations. If they wanted to keep pure and avoid falling into sexual immorality, Paul's advice was simple—get married.

However, Paul's advice does not mean that a single man or woman should go out looking for someone to marry. Think about it. Where does God's plan come into view for your life? If you are single, pray about marriage and who you are to marry. Wait on God for His best. Many single people have an idea of what they want in a spouse. A young man may decide he wants to marry a beautiful girl with all the right dimensions, and a young woman desires a well-built, handsome man.

Marriage is much more than just the outer appearance of a person. What about the heart? What is their character like? Single people need to be more concerned that they are in the perfect will of God; otherwise, they will find marriage to be a great disappointment. It is important to marry God's chosen person for you. Marriage can be a blessing—heaven on earth—or it can be hell on earth!

Men and women need to nail their passions to the Cross—denying themselves—before they make a lifelong decision: *Pursue...holiness, without which no one will see the Lord* (Hebrews 12:14).

An intimate close relationship with Jesus Christ through prayer and His Word will keep you from sin. Listen to the wisdom of the psalmist:

> *How can a young man cleanse his way? By taking heed according to Your word. With my whole heart I have sought You; oh, let me not wander from Your commandments! Your word I have hidden in my heart, that I might not sin against You.*

> PSALM 119:9-11

A Duty to Love

> *Let the husband render to his wife the affection due her, and likewise also the wife to her husband. The wife does not have authority over her own body, but the husband does. And likewise the husband does not have authority over his own body, but the wife does.*

> 1 CORINTHIANS 7:3-4

Paul continued to speak on the subject of marriage. It is a husband's duty to love his wife and show her marital affection, and likewise the wife toward her husband.

If the husband is not the spiritual leader of the home, I guarantee there will be problems. Husbands are to love their wives, and then the wife will naturally submit to his loving leadership:

> *Husbands, love your wives, just as Christ also loved the church and gave Himself for her, that He might sanctify and cleanse her with the washing of water by the word, that He might present her to Himself a glorious church, not having spot or wrinkle or any such thing, but that she should be holy and without blemish. So husbands ought to love their own wives as their own bodies; he who loves his wife loves himself. For no one ever hated his own flesh, but nourishes and cherishes it, just as the Lord does the church... Nevertheless let each one of you in particular so*

love his own wife as himself, and let the wife see that she respects her husband.

EPHESIANS 5:25-29, 33

If a wife feels unloved, she may go elsewhere for affection. She needs her husband to give her loving attention and to be told she surpasses all other women. Some wives like flowers and little gifts. Others like to be held—caressed. If you show love to your wife, that will keep the temperature of your marriage. When you love and cherish her, she will respect you.

After marriage, some people can become unsatisfied—things may change. If a husband has watched pornography or other things on television and social media, he is sure to become unsatisfied with his wife. It could be that he is fantasizing and allowing his mind to be seduced. Satan is very clever; when he sees a weakness in a marriage relationship, he will bring someone along to tempt a husband or wife into committing adultery.

A spouse may think they are just joking and talking with a person of the opposite sex. Things may begin innocently enough, but then it can turn into giving each other compliments. A husband can tell his wife that the girl he has been speaking with is just a friend. They are just talking, and there is nothing going on. Let me tell you, that is very naïve—opposite sexes attract. The enemy works to tempt two people to get together, and then they fall into adultery—it happens. The problem is often a lack of self-control. Be careful—be blameless.

6

CHRISTIAN LIFE LESSONS

MATTHEW 5:33-48

Jesus continued His discourse to all those who had gathered to Him. He spoke on the subject of integrity—keeping oaths and not swearing falsely. Once again, the Lord reverted back to the Law. Jesus knew the scribes, Sadducees and Pharisees had taken the Law of God with the intent to misuse, distort, pollute and twist it—to bring God's people into bondage. So Jesus referred to Old Testament Scriptures and then taught it with the right intent.

KEEPING YOUR OATHS — Matthew 5:33-37

> "Again you have heard that it was said to those of old, 'You shall not swear falsely, but shall perform your oaths to the Lord.' But I say to you, do not swear at all: neither by heaven, for it is God's throne; nor by the earth, for it is His footstool; nor by Jerusalem, for it is the city of the great King. Nor shall you swear by your head, because you cannot make one hair white or black. But let your 'Yes' be 'Yes,' and your 'No,' 'No.' For whatever is more than these is from the evil one."

In the Old Testament, making an oath before the Lord was a serious subject. An oath spoken before God was a declaration made in truth

81

as an appeal to Him. Oaths made from a person's heart inwardly, with sincere intentions, were to be kept:

> *"If a man makes a vow to the LORD, or swears an oath to bind himself by some agreement, he shall not break his word; he shall do according to all that proceeds out of his mouth."*

NUMBERS 30:2

God expected a person to keep their vows and oaths made to Him. It is a sin to make a vow to God and not pay it:

> *"When you make a vow to the LORD your God, you shall not delay to pay it; for the LORD your God will surely require it of you, and it would be sin to you. But if you abstain from vowing, it shall not be sin to you."*

DEUTERONOMY 23:21-22

King Solomon was gifted with God's wisdom. He advised: *When you make a vow to God, do not delay to pay it; for He has no pleasure in fools. Pay what you have vowed—better not to vow than to vow and not pay* (Ecclesiastes 5:4-5).

When Christians make promises to God, they act foolishly when they do not keep their vow. God holds them accountable. He expects them to keep their promises. Do not make a false vow to God, do not lie, and make sure you speak the truth before Him.

Swearing Falsely

Jesus resolved the issue of people making oaths and not keeping them. He taught them not to swear at all. They should not swear by heaven, earth, Jerusalem, nor by their heads! In fact, this type of swearing was considered as using God's name in vain.

Many people swear and make promises, but they do not keep their oaths given to men, much less oaths given to God. This is swearing falsely. In the Ten Commandments, God strictly warned: *"You shall not take the name of the LORD your God in vain, for the LORD will not hold him guiltless who takes His name in vain"* (Exodus 20:7).

In today's society, jurors swear on the Holy Bible before the court, saying, "I do solemnly swear to tell the truth, the whole truth, and nothing but the truth, so help me God!" Other people use the name of God so lightly. His holy name is used in pure ignorance as a common, slang, curse word. The common phrase, "I swear to God," is often used as a promise to another person that their word is true, and it will be kept. Those who borrow money promise, "If you lend me $100.00, I swear to God, I will pay you back."

God also commanded His people: " *'And you shall not swear by My name falsely, nor shall you profane the name of your God: I am the LORD'* " (Leviticus 19:12). Stop using God's name in vain! Be careful with your speech! Those who use God's name in vain will stand guilty before a holy God on Judgment Day!

The intent of God's Law was to keep a person from dishonoring God by falsely calling upon His name or cursing Him. It protected a man from perjuring himself— showing himself to be a liar or an unjust and unstable person. It also guarded against treating others unjustly or swearing a lie to cover the truth.

Instead of swearing falsely, Jesus gave His disciples an easy principle to follow: *"...let your 'Yes' be 'Yes,' and your 'No,' 'No.' "* In doing so, Jesus corrected any false ideas about the Law and illustrated the superiority of a person's inward heart. The true implication of God's Law regarding an oath is that words spoken should be kept in sincerity. The word *sincerity* means "the appearance and reality are exactly the same." Whatever you promise someone, that is exactly what you are going to do.

Sadly, at the present time, there are still a lot of Christians who do not keep their word. Nonbelievers complain, "Can you really trust a Christian?" Every Sunday they see believers go off to church carrying

THE SERMON OF SERMONS

their Bibles, but because of what they say and fail to do, nonbelievers see them as walking contradictions.

People find it extremely annoying when someone makes a promise to them, and they do not keep their word. A disciple of Christ should always keep their word. Can people trust what you say? Make good on what you have promised. Be a man or a woman of your word. Let your word be your bond!

Promises Made, Promises Kept

People make promises, and their promises need to be kept. God's Word holds a person accountable: "*That which has gone from your lips you shall keep and perform, for you voluntarily vowed to the* LORD *your God what you have promised with your mouth*" (Deuteronomy 23:23). If you are going to make a promise to someone, then fear God, because as a Christian, you are a debtor to that given promise. Christians represent the Lord to others. Any promises made have to be kept—fully and completely.

How many people get into credit card debt? In America, statistics record that the average household credit card debt is $5,315.00. People can get into trouble when they treat credit cards as cash. Whatever amount is borrowed has a high interest rate. Some cards charge as much as 25%. Consumer debt in the U.S., for mortgages, auto loans, credit cards and student loans, stands at an incredible $14.9 trillion! Both men and women are guilty of making purchases without paying back creditors as promised. People rack up debt and fail to make good on their word. After spending what they cannot really afford, some of them declare bankruptcy. That is not right. Creditors trust a person to pay back any money owed. My motto is, "If you cannot afford it, do not buy it." It is best not to be in debt to anyone. Be wise—so important.

Maybe you are a person who has not kept your promises. Know that Satan will always tempt you to lie and not to keep your word. Believers in Christ can no longer walk in darkness or be liars. Apply to your life an exhortation given by the Apostle Paul to the believers in Colossae:

Do not lie to one another, since you have put off the old man with his deeds, and have put on the new man who is renewed in knowledge according to the image of Him who created him...

COLOSSIANS 3:9-10

Be honest; keep your word. Do what you have said, not only to God, but to others. It is important not to bring a bad name to the Gospel of Jesus Christ by any sinful behavior. Christian men and women must have integrity. If believers are going to live for Christ, they need to practice what they preach!

Jesus, in His sermon, trained His disciples using biblical principles that cannot be changed. As a Christian, determine in your heart to live by the sermon He taught in the Scriptures. Otherwise, if you fail to obey Christ's words, you will never make a strong impact in the lives of those within your home, among your loved ones and friends, or even in the nation in which you live.

THE LAW OF RETRIBUTION — Matthew 5:38-42

"You have heard that it was said, 'An eye for an eye and a tooth for a tooth.' But I tell you not to resist an evil person. But whoever slaps you on your right cheek, turn the other to him also. If anyone wants to sue you and take away your tunic, let him have your cloak also. And whoever compels you to go one mile, go with him two. Give to him who asks you, and from him who wants to borrow from you do not turn away."

In the Old Testament, God established the Law of retribution. When an offense was committed against another person, instead of mercy, the rule to live by was pure retaliation:

> *"...you shall give life for life, eye for eye, tooth for tooth, hand for hand, foot for foot, burn for burn, wound for wound, stripe for stripe."*

EXODUS 21:23-25

> *" 'If a man causes disfigurement of his neighbor, as he has done, so shall it be done to him—fracture for fracture, eye for eye, tooth for tooth; as he has caused disfigurement of a man, so shall it be done to him.' "*

LEVITICUS 24:19-20

> *"...Your eye shall not pity: life shall be for life, eye for eye, tooth for tooth, hand for hand, foot for foot."*

DEUTERONOMY 19:21

Over the centuries, the Law of retribution has been abused and misused. Men were merciless. They decided to use this Law to excuse themselves for treating people however they wished. In actuality, the purpose of the Law was to show mercy and not vengeance. The Law did not have to be executed. The Law allowed a person some justice if they wished, but justice was limited to an equivalent injury. The Law of retribution was given to the courts to guide judges in their execution of justice. They were not given to individuals to forcibly take vengeance into their own hands, but to do what was right according to the Scriptures.

Jesus quoted from the Old Testament Law of retribution, but because of the grace of God in the New Testament, in His authority, He changed it. Notice how Jesus once again used the phrase, *"but I say to you."* He continued teaching that His disciples were not to retaliate. Instead, they were to arm themselves with the right attitude toward any person who acted unreasonably toward them or had evil intentions. It would take humility to humble themselves before a person who had wronged them—to show them Christ's love.

Jesus taught His disciples, *"But whoever slaps you on your right cheek, turn the other to him also."* A slap on the face was, and continues to be, a serious insult. When slapped on the cheek, it was natural for anyone to retaliate, but followers of Jesus Christ were to turn the other cheek and not seek revenge. The principle meaning of Christ's teaching was to show another person mercy. Any offense should be forgiven. When a believer chose not to retaliate, this did not mean they were weak; it signified they had the character of Christ—meekness—power under control.

Christians are to follow the example of Christ. Jesus exercised meekness when arrested, bound and questioned by the Jews. The High Priest asked Jesus about His disciples and His doctrine. Jesus redirected the question, saying,

> *"I spoke openly to the world. I always taught in synagogues and in the temple, where the Jews always meet, and in secret I have said nothing. Why do you ask Me? Ask those who have heard Me what I said to them. Indeed they know what I said."*

> JOHN 18:20-21

Immediately, one of the officers struck Jesus with the palm of his hand. Jesus did not retaliate, but said to him, *"If I have spoken evil, bear witness of the evil; but if well, why do you strike Me?"* (John 18:23). Can you imagine, if the officer remained unrepentant for striking Jesus, what would happen to him when he stands before Christ on Judgment Day?

It is hard to be spirit-controlled, especially when someone is insulting, defaming, mocking or intentionally pushing your buttons. Many times, I have failed. We have a sinful nature that desires to retaliate, but we are not to meet anger with anger. Have a Christ-like attitude, and take to heart the Apostle Paul's exhortation: *Do not be overcome by evil, but overcome evil with good* (Romans 12:21).

A person may feel they are justified when they retaliate. They give themselves an excuse because they feel they have a valid reason to retaliate; but as long as their life is not in danger, it is better to forgive, to be Christ-like. In doing so, you are showing Christ's love.

Retaliation within Families

I believe with all my heart that retaliating against someone in your family is one of the worst forms of wickedness. A husband can retaliate by deliberately not talking to his wife. A spouse who has suffered abuse or feels betrayed by a divorce can retaliate and take their pain out on others. A parent can cruelly cut off a child, or a child, a parent. Sometimes, out of spite, people physically hurt another family member. The Lord does not want families to retaliate against each other, but to love and forgive.

As a child of God, there is no good reason why you cannot choose to love and forgive. If you are seeking to retaliate, how do you expect the Holy Spirit to move in your life? You cannot harbor any bitterness or anger in your heart. When you disobey the Word of God, you willfully transgress. The problem is always disobedience. May the Holy Spirit convict you!

Go the Extra Mile

Jesus knew His audience and the times in which they lived. Individually, any person could suffer because of unreasonable demands asked of them. The Romans occupied Israel, and the Jews hated them. A Roman soldier could tap any Jewish citizen on the shoulder with his sword and demand that they carry his pack for a mile. It weighed as much as 66 pounds! Jesus taught His disciples the right response: "*And whoever compels you to go one mile, go with him two*" (Matthew 5:41). They should go far and beyond what was asked of them—go the extra mile!

If a disciple had the right attitude, they would not be blinded by resentment or anger; instead they would see the situation as an open opportunity to share Christ. They could be a good witness. Imagine the soldier's response!

If a Christian became angry and resentful, they would lose the blessing of bringing a person to Jesus Christ who needed salvation. Again, it takes humility and love to respond the right way. Living by these Christ-like attitudes and actions will testify that you are indeed a disciple of Christ!

Jesus Christ was not saying to never stand up and resist evil. There is a time for righteous anger. Jesus showed righteous anger when He turned over the tables of the money changers in the Temple. The priests were ripping off the people. Jesus was angry, which was not resentment or retaliation. He took a whip and chased these men out of the Temple, saying, *"It is written, 'My house shall be called a house of prayer,' but you have made it a 'den of thieves' "* (Matthew 21:12-13). There is a time and place for godly anger.

Christian Graces

Jesus took the principle of giving one step further to show His disciples true Christian graces—mercy, love, kindness and goodness. Jesus taught: *"If anyone wants to sue you and take away your tunic, let him have your cloak also...Give to him who asks you, and from him who wants to borrow from you do not turn away"* (Matthew 5:40, 42). The right response to anyone who unfairly sued them for their inner tunic, an undergarment, was to give away their outer garment, a cloak, as well.

Under the Law of Moses, if an outer cloak was given in a pledge, it should not be permanently kept; it was to be returned to the owner. A cloak was a meticulously woven garment. It was very valuable and indispensable. At night a person would use a cloak as a covering to sleep under:

> *"If the neighbor is poor, do not go to sleep with their pledge in your possession. Return their cloak by sunset so that your*

neighbor may sleep in it. Then they will thank you, and it will be regarded as a righteous act in the sight of the LORD your God."

DEUTERONOMY 24:12-13 (NIV)

Although legally, according to the Law, a person could keep their cloak, Jesus told His disciples to give this valued possession away. They were to let them have the cloak because it was more important to resolve the hostile situation.

Think of all the unpleasant lawsuits happening among Christians. It was Paul the Apostle who exhorted believers to settle their issues out of court. Christians are supposed to be *salt* and *light*. Even families sue each other—sad. What kind of witness is that to your loved ones, friends, and those in the world? Believers should not have a bad testimony. However, if a person is suing you unrighteously, then you need to defend yourself by going to court. Get a good defense lawyer!

LOVE YOUR ENEMIES — Matthew 5:43-45

> "You have heard that it was said, 'You shall love your neighbor and hate your enemy.' But I say to you, love your enemies, bless those who curse you, do good to those who hate you, and pray for those who spitefully use you and persecute you, that you may be sons of your Father in heaven; for He makes His sun rise on the evil and on the good, and sends rain on the just and on the unjust."

In the Old Testament, we can read how the Law was instituted and intended to operate. However, the Pharisees added to the Law of God. For instance, in Leviticus 19:18, nothing was said about hating an enemy. The Law simply stated: " '...*love your neighbor as yourself...*' " Jewish leaders decided to interpret this Law as loving their own people, religion and nation. In other words, by adding "...*and hate your enemy,*" they made it their purpose to hate people!

Jesus desired to extend grace to mankind. In His authority, He explained to His followers the true intent of the Law. He began by saying, *"You have heard it said,"* and then changed it to, *"But I say to you, love your enemies."* Even though people were accustomed to hating their enemies, Jesus taught them to love. In doing so, Jesus corrected the Pharisees. They had made a fatal mistake in interpreting the Law. God is not hateful toward anyone. God is love. People make the choice to love or hate, but a true child of God knows the character of His Creator, and they must choose to love others, which is a hard thing to do.

When Jesus taught His followers *"love your enemies,"* He used the Greek word *agápe*. This type of love is a deep, unconditional love. It is a love of the mind, reason and choice. God's *agápe* love is sacrificial. It is a love that genuinely cares for people. Jesus, the Son of God, deliberately chose *agápe* love when He died on the Cross to show to the world that He loved mankind (John 3:16), even to the extent of forgiving His enemies while dying on the Cross. He said, *"Father, forgive them, for they do not know what they do"* (Luke 23:34).

Christians are to imitate Christ. They will win people to Jesus Christ by demonstrating humility and the love of Christ to them. In fulfilling the Old Testament Scriptures, Jesus explained in the New Testament that instead of retaliating, His disciples were to bless people.

A Christian's good works are to be done for the benefit of others, no matter how they respond. *Agápe* love is always giving and forgiving. Christ's love involves very practical acts:

> *Love suffers long and is kind; love does not envy; love does not parade itself, is not puffed up; does not behave rudely, does not seek its own, is not provoked, thinks no evil; does not rejoice in iniquity, but rejoices in the truth; bears all things, believes all things, hopes all things, endures all things. Love never fails.*

> 1 CORINTHIANS 13:4-8

Pray and ask God to give you sacrificial love for a person you dislike. When they stand before you, and you choose to show God's *agápe* love toward them instead of hate, they will be shocked! *Agápe* love is not a phony love. It is a love that causes you to go the extra mile to *"bless those who curse you, do good to those who hate you, and pray for those who spitefully use you and persecute you"* (Matthew 5:44).

After the Vietnam War ended in 1973, I harbored a lot of hate toward my enemies. People often say, time can heal pain. I agree, but still I remember and grieve over many of my friends who were killed in the war. As time passed, in 2007 the Lord opened the door for me to return to Vietnam. When I first met with those men I called enemies, Jesus' words in the Sermon on the Mount came into my mind, *"Love your enemies."* Through Christ, those I once called enemies, I now call friends. I can truly say that returning to Vietnam and shaking the hands of my enemies in friendship were moments I truly practiced Christianity.

As a Christian, you may think, *How can I love and pray for someone who has stabbed me in the back, talked about me, or has hurt my spouse or children?* I know it is very hard, but this is the Christian attitude that we are to have. In our old, sinful nature, we want to retaliate and get revenge, but we must forgive and pray for those who have hurt us. This is impossible without Christ and the enabling power of the Holy Spirit.

How do you know for sure that you have truly forgiven someone? I believe, when you see or think about them, there will no longer be any ill feelings or physical anger that suddenly arises in your heart. Whatever happened in the past is left in the hands of the Lord. When you obey what Jesus has taught you, and you put God's love into practice, your actions will bring you peace. Then you will know God is working in your life.

You can read the Bible all you want, but it is your actions and attitudes that count. Your heart's desire for your enemies and anyone who has hurt you must be to see them saved.

A Lack of Love

As I travel the country, I see that love is lacking in the Church. Listen to Jesus. He placed great emphasis on love in the Church. Love is an identifying factor in the life of His disciples:

"A new commandment I give to you, that you love one another; as I have loved you, that you also love one another. By this all will know that you are My disciples, if you have love for one another."

JOHN 13:34-35

A Christian's love shows they are distinct from all other people. Love is the evidence of a real disciple of Christ. God's love is working in and through them. As believers, we strive to become more like Christ— to *pursue righteousness, godliness, faith, love, patience, gentleness* (1 Timothy 6:11). These are true spiritual fruits. Christians love people.

I was saved through the power of God's love. It transformed my life, and I became a new person. The Holy Spirit brought conviction to my life. I knew the Holy Spirit was real! He caused me to love and forgive my parents, and they saw an incredible difference in my life. Are you aware that the Holy Spirit is real in your life? Is there a complete change of heart? Are you listening or ignoring what the Holy Spirit is saying to you?

THE PATTERN OF PERFECTION — Matthew 5:46-48

"For if you love those who love you, what reward have you? Do not even the tax collectors do the same? And if you greet your brethren only, what do you do more than others? Do not even the tax collectors do so? Therefore you shall be perfect, just as your Father in heaven is perfect."

Jesus first stated the obvious in His sermon. Even tax collectors, those whom the Jews abhorred, loved people who loved them back. They naturally returned love. What reward was there in that? There was no real difference between a disciple of Christ and the nonbeliever. It was very easy to love someone who loved them in return. Jesus gave His disciples a different pattern to follow—to go far beyond what others ordinarily did! Love an enemy, someone who had inflicted hurt—now that was difficult!

Jesus set a high standard for His followers: *"...be perfect, just as your Father in heaven is perfect."* How can a Christian be perfect? Nobody is perfect—none of us. Perfection does not mean being without sin. The word *perfect* means "mature." It points to a particular stage of Christian growth—a full development of maturity—godliness, and this can only happen through Christ who dwells in us.

When a person is saved, they are not perfect. Believers will fail, trip, fall and get back up. When a believer is educated in the Word of God, and the Holy Spirit is actively working in his life, he desires to be in God's perfect will, and he will become a spiritual person—obedient to God. However, there are so-called Christians who want to play church. They hear a sermon, but they do not live the sermon. True Christians obey the Word of God.

Christians develop spiritually by reading, praying and building a relationship with Jesus Christ: *...till we all come to the unity of the faith and of the knowledge of the Son of God, to a perfect* [mature] *man, to the measure of the stature of the fullness of Christ...* (Ephesians 4:13).

Again, *perfect* means "mature": *But let patience have its perfect work, that you may be perfect* [mature] *and complete, lacking nothing* (James 1:4). Christian believers are to mature into holiness:*...beloved, let us cleanse ourselves from all filthiness of the flesh and spirit, perfecting holiness in the fear of God* (2 Corinthians 7:1). Aim to be perfect; progress, and do not digress. It is important to move forward and not backward.

The mature Christian is a person who will do good and show kindness to people whether they are good or bad. Make it a goal to love and forgive people. Then those in the world can see a marked difference—that you are a child of God.

God's Amazing Grace

There is no way Christians can attain perfection. Jesus' words cause us to see the need for God's grace to be actively working in our lives. Christians need God's amazing grace—His unmerited favor—because they daily fail in their attempts to love others and be like Christ. They struggle with their sinful nature, for without God, they can do nothing (John 15:5). God is the only One who can help build our Christian character. He sanctifies us—sets us apart. A. W. Tozer drills this important thought into our minds:

> We please Him most, not by frantically trying to make ourselves good, but by throwing ourselves into His arms with all our imperfections and believing that He understands everything and still loves us.[3]

During the day, a believer can have evil thoughts and commit evil actions; and by the time they go to bed, if it were not for the grace of God, they would be condemned to eternal destruction!

Disciples of Christ need to understand the grace of God; it speaks of their position in Christ. His grace will keep them as they pray and ask God for the forgiveness of their sins each day: *If we confess our sins, He is faithful and just to forgive us our sins and to cleanse us from all unrighteousness* (1 John 1:9).

Obedience and a reverent fear of God are important in the Christian life. Serve God with the understanding that no one hides from what they do in secret—in the darkness. Always take God's Word at face value:

> *Therefore, my beloved, as you have always obeyed, not as in my presence only, but now much more in my absence, work out your*

own salvation with fear and trembling; for it is God who works in you both to will and to do for His good pleasure.

PHILIPPIANS 2:12-13

We need God's grace, His wisdom and knowledge, His power and anointing, and His leading and guidance in our lives. Believers are warned by God's Spirit not to commit sin. They have the conviction and the power of the Holy Spirit to help direct their lives: "*But the Helper, the Holy Spirit, whom the Father will send in My name, He will teach you all things, and bring to your remembrance all things that I said to you*" (John 14:26).

With the enablement of the Holy Spirit, always pursue the high standard—to be perfect, just as your Father in heaven is perfect. Keep this in mind: one day, in heaven, we shall be perfect!

7

A LIFE PLEASING TO GOD

MATTHEW 6:1-8

Disciples of Christ are to live a life pleasing to God in every area of their lives. Jesus addressed a specific area in which they needed to be pleasing to God—their charitable deeds—giving. Jesus began by saying to His followers, *"Take heed."* This meant they were to "pay special attention," as He was just about to say something of great importance.

PUBLICIZED CHARITABLE DEEDS — Matthew 6:1-2

"Take heed that you do not do your charitable deeds before men, to be seen by them. Otherwise you have no reward from your Father in heaven. Therefore, when you do a charitable deed, do not sound a trumpet before you as the hypocrites do in the synagogues and in the streets, that they may have glory from men. Assuredly, I say to you, they have their reward."

Jesus openly taught His disciples the right way to give. They were to give sacrificially, without drawing attention to themselves. Nobody should see what they gave. He taught them the right way to give—to be pleasing to God, not to men. Otherwise, they would have no reward from their Father in heaven.

Jesus referred to *hypocrites*; these were the self-righteous Pharisees who appeared to be something they were obviously not. His disciples were not to be like them. When the Pharisees gave their offerings to God, they purposely drew people's attention to themselves. They would place their monetary gifts in little boxes and drop them into the treasury to make a loud clanging sound. In the temple, they would even blow the shofar—a ram's horn that made a sound of a trumpet—all because they desired recognition. Imagine, in a place of true worship, the Pharisees blew their own horn!

The Pharisees must have thought to themselves, *How spiritual and marvelous I am in my giving to God.* They wanted to impress people and let them know just how spiritual they were. They loved to receive all the praise from men. That was their earthly reward; they would receive no heavenly reward.

In comparison, Jesus drew His disciples' attention to a little widow. When she gave her offering, it was just a tiny mite. Jesus told His disciples the widow had given more than the Pharisees because she had given her all—all that she had! Giving is never about the amount, but the sacrifice behind the gift. The widow had a genuine motive to please God, and in doing so, she drew no attention to herself.

Pharisaical hypocrisy exists in the Church. There are people who make themselves look super-spiritual when giving to the Lord. All they desire is recognition and to be seen by men. They love to be patted on the back for their generous giving. Giving for recognition is a characteristic of a hypocrite. Christians cannot become like the Pharisees—hypocrites. Believers must guard their hearts and be alert to the deception of giving to be seen by men.

When giving to the Lord, offerings should not be hand-held-high and waved to bring attention to the giver. No one should see how much an individual person gives in the church offering. People who choose man's rewards receive the poorest reward. They actually cheat themselves out of what God intended to give them.

A person may give for self-satisfaction or self-admiration. They may give out of obligation or out of a sense of duty; or may give to feel that they have scored with God. Think about that. Yet God knows every single motive in their acts of giving. In the kingdom of God, those who have given with wrong motives will lose their reward. They will receive nothing!

Make sure you remember what Christ has taught you in His sermon about giving and check your motives. Are your motives hypocritical or genuine? I believe with all my heart that before Christians give financially to the Lord or others, they first need to examine their hearts. Why are they giving? Who are they doing it for? What is their attitude? Are their charitable deeds accomplished with a humble and giving spirit?

One day, every single one of us will stand before the Bema seat of Christ to give an account for things we have done on earth, whether good or bad (2 Corinthians 5:10-12). Knowing this, the Apostle Paul gave us this lifetime aim: *Therefore we make it our aim, whether present or absent, to be well pleasing to Him* [God] (2 Corinthians 5:9). Again, the true motive for giving is to be pleasing to God.

SECRET CHARITABLE DEEDS — Matthew 6:3-4

"But when you do a charitable deed [alms], do not let your left hand know what your right hand is doing, that your charitable deed may be in secret; and your Father who sees in secret will Himself reward you openly."

The Jewish people had three important duties toward God: giving, praying and fasting. Giving alms was a righteous act done to meet the needs of the poor: " *'If one of your brethren becomes poor, and falls into poverty among you, then you shall help him, like a stranger or a sojourner, that he may live with you'* " (Leviticus 25:35).

In the written Law of God, Jews understood their responsibility to be generous toward the poor: *"If there is among you a poor man of your brethren, within any of the gates in your land which the LORD your God is giving you, you shall not harden your heart nor shut your hand from your poor brother..."* (Deuteronomy 15:7). Giving alms was one of the greatest things a Jew could do, but they often did these charitable acts openly to be seen of men.

Jesus taught the fundamentals of doing charitable deeds in secret—not letting your left hand know what your right hand is doing. Nothing passes God's attention. God is the one who sees what is given secretly, and He is the one who rewards us openly. No one else can reward us. God may not always reward us financially, but He can bless us in other ways; He can reward us spiritually.

Once again, Jesus instilled in His followers the right way to give. Whatever they did in helping someone, they were to make sure it was for God's glory alone. He was the One to receive all the glory for any charitable deeds they accomplished.

In your giving you must act in humility, with pure motives, and the Lord will honor you. God will greatly use a person's life when they learn to give in secret with the right attitude. They have become men and women of integrity. God sees their genuine heart of generosity and rewards them openly. I like that! A. W. Tozer gave an amazing insight into why we should give in secret and resist seeking the spotlight:

> There is a tendency to seek the spotlight when helping others so that recognition and commendation are ours. But blessed is the helper who helps the one in need secretly or unobtrusively. Such help is easier to accept and of it God is fully aware.

The Apostle Paul addressed a Christian's charitableness by simply reminding believers of Jesus' own words, along with his example to them: *"I have shown you in every way, by laboring like this, that you must support the weak. And remember the words of the Lord Jesus, that He said, 'It is more blessed to give than to receive'* " (Acts 20:35). Paul taught the responsibility of giving to the poor without expecting anything in return—so important.

Have you ever experienced the blessing of giving financially to the Lord and to others in secret? God wants us to be loving, kind and generous. When was the last time you bought a meal for someone on the street? We need to help the needy, especially if we have been blessed with abundance financially.

Giving Offerings to God

In Deuteronomy 16:17, God's people were instructed in giving to God: *"Every man shall give as he is able, according to the blessing of the LORD your God which He has given you."* In the New Testament, we find the Apostle Paul's instructions: *On the first day of the week let each one of you lay something aside, storing up as he may prosper...* (1 Corinthians 16:2). Christians must be obedient to God in giving offerings. Give regularly, every Sunday morning, as the Lord directs you, from all He has blessed you with throughout the week.

When people are taught biblical principles in giving, it helps them to learn the right way to give to God. Christians are to pray about what to give sacrificially to the Lord. Paul taught believers: *So let each one give as he purposes in his heart, not grudgingly or of necessity; for God loves a cheerful giver.* (2 Corinthians 9:7).

Believers in Christ are to give hilariously and joyfully to the Lord! We should never begrudge giving to God. It is because of people's obedient and cheerful giving that we have been able to maintain our own home church and build Bible schools in South America. I have learned from Pastor Chuck Smith, "Where God guides, God provides." God provides through His people when they obediently give. God does not need our support, but He does require our obedience.

Abundant Giving

In the book of Exodus, in the project of building the sanctuary, the people's hearts were moved to bring to Moses their freewill offerings. The people gave sacrificially and in such abundance that Moses had to restrain them from giving:

> *So Moses gave a commandment, and they caused it to be proclaimed throughout the camp, saying, "Let neither man nor woman do any more work for the offering of the sanctuary." And the people were restrained from bringing, for the material they had was sufficient for all the work to be done—indeed too much.*

EXODUS 36:6-7

I can imagine Moses saying, "Thank you for giving!" The Lord was pleased with their giving. We do not hear about that kind of giving in churches today! In fact, many Christians are disobedient to the Word of God, and they do not give. What about you? Is God pleased with your obedient giving?

The motive behind our giving is obedience to the Word of God. We give to God sacrificially, because of all that He has done for us! If there is no obedient giving, how can churches get the Gospel out to a world that is lost? If God's work is to be accomplished, then believers must learn to give to the Lord sacrificially. Imagine, if every person obediently gave to God what belongs to God, then what great things the Church could do with the Gospel—incredible!

In the Gospel of Luke, the Sermon on the Mount is also recorded. Jesus taught another good principle about giving from there:

> *"Give, and it will be given to you: good measure, pressed down, shaken together, and running over will be put into your bosom. For with the same measure that you use, it will be measured back to you."*

LUKE 6:38

Pastor Chuck Smith explains:

> "Give: it's a principle; it's a spiritual law. We've learned to observe natural laws and live by them and profit from them, but we ought also to learn the spiritual laws, and this is a spiritual law; it works. You say, 'I don't know how it can work.' I don't know either, but I know it does. Whatever measure you mete, it shall be measured to you. So in giving, the Lord will give back to you on whatever measure you give. However, He will give back more. Because He will give out, good measure, pressed down, shaken together, running over."

So give God your best, not your castoffs, and become a channel of blessing to others.

Holes in Money Bags

In the book of Haggai, the Jews had left Babylon and returned to their own land. The protective wall around Jerusalem and the Jewish temple needed rebuilding, but the people were far too busy building their own beautiful, paneled houses. God's people had selfish priorities, and they failed to obediently give to the Lord. This disobedience had disastrous consequences.

As God's people sold their crops and earned wages, they placed their earnings in money bags and buried them for safe keeping, but the Lord told them:

> *"You have sown much, and bring in little; you eat, but do not have enough; you drink, but you are not filled with drink; you clothe yourselves, but no one is warm; and he who earns wages, earns wages to put into a bag with holes."*

> HAGGAI 1:6

The more God's people made financially, the more He took! Perhaps the reason people in church have financial problems is because they have selfish priorities. They have failed to give to God what belongs to God. Listen and learn from what God had to say to His people:

> *"Will a man rob God? Yet you have robbed Me! But you say, 'In what way have we robbed You?' In tithes and offerings. You are cursed with a curse, for you have robbed Me, even this whole nation. Bring all the tithes into the storehouse, that there may be food in My house, and try Me now in this," says the* Lord *of hosts, "If I will not open for you the windows of heaven and pour out for you such blessing that there will not be room enough to receive it. And I will rebuke the devourer for your sakes, so that he will not destroy the fruit of your ground, nor shall the vine fail to bear fruit for you in the field," says the* Lord *of hosts; "And all nations will call you blessed, for you will be a delightful land," says the* Lord *of hosts.*

MALACHI 3:8-12

I believe that giving is an area where the Church is failing. If God has blessed you, how sad it is not to give! Why not memorize this quote by C. T. Studd to help you keep the right perspective in your giving:

> "Only one life, 'twill soon be past, Only what's done for Christ will last."

Our heart's desire should always be to hear the Lord's voice saying to us in eternity, " *'Well done, good and faithful servant; you were faithful over a few things, I will make you ruler over many things. Enter into the joy of your lord'* " (Matthew 25:21).

INSINCERE PRAYERS — Matthew 6:5

"And when you pray, you shall not be like the hypocrites. For they love to pray standing in the synagogues and on the corners of the streets, that they may be seen by men. Assuredly, I say to you, they have their reward."

Jesus expanded His description of hypocrites. They prayed in public to be seen by men, standing in the synagogues and on the street corners—hands lifted high—praying out loud. People thought they were so spiritual, but the praise and recognition of men was their reward.

Jesus instructed His listeners on the right way to pray; they should not draw attention to themselves. His lengthy sermon developed right heart attitudes concerning giving, praying and fasting. These three important elements are central to the Christian's life.

So why is it that in the congregation, we sometimes find people who stand up in the front rows with their arms lifted high to pray while the rest of the congregation is sitting? Is their motive to be seen by men? Who are they trying to impress, those sitting around them? I believe that in most instances, those standing usually want to gain man's attention.

People know in their hearts that if they stand up in a front row to worship or pray, everyone else behind them is going to think how spiritual they are. God is not honored. However, it could be a person may stand up to worship or pray in sincerity; then God is honored.

In group prayer, everyone's heart motives need to be right. Each person waits to pray, and everyone's prayer is different. Prayer is not so a person can impress others. Have you heard certain individuals change their voices when they pray to very high pitched or extremely low tones? When they make such a pretense in praying, others will focus on listening to them, and their minds and hearts will be taken away from the Lord.

At times, some people pray out loud to voice a personal vendetta. It is usually an attempt to convict someone else in the group. I believe people can tell when this is happening. It is obvious that these people are not addressing God, but an individual in the group.

There are Christians who, instead of sincerely praying, try to preach a message—a sermon. Their prayers are so longwinded that they do not allow others in the group time to pray. Humorously, Charles Spurgeon had this to say: "It is necessary to draw near unto God, but it is not required of you to prolong your speech till everyone is longing to hear the word 'Amen'. "

Christians need to be careful how they pray. Our prayers should not be too long or overly spiritual. When we pray to God, our prayers should be sincere—straight from our hearts. Well-known preacher Alan Redpath gave this helpful admonition:

> Prayer opens the channel between a soul and God; prayerlessness closes it. Prayer releases the grip of Satan's power; prayerlessness increases it. That is why prayer is so exhausting and so vital. If we believed it, the prayer meeting would be as full as the church.

Before praying to God, make sure your heart is right before Him. Ask yourself, *What is my motive in coming before the throne of grace?* When joining in prayer with others, forget about yourself; be a good prayer warrior—close to the heart of God.

PRAYING IN SECRET — Matthew 6:6-8

> "But you, when you pray, go into your room, and when you have shut your door, pray to your Father who is in the secret place; and your Father who sees in secret will reward you openly. And when you pray, do not use vain repetitions as the heathen do. For they think that they will be heard for their many words. Therefore do not be like them. For your Father knows the things you have need of before you ask Him."

Jesus placed such a great emphasis on how His disciples should pray. He wanted them to understand the necessity and the benefits of praying in secret. They needed a secluded place where no one else could see or hear them. When they came before God's throne room of grace, they could pray in complete privacy, quietly, without drawing attention to themselves. In a place such as this there would be no distractions.

Many people make the mistake of praying prayers repetitiously. Jesus taught His disciples the exact opposite. They should not use vain, empty repetitions. God may hear loud, long, repetitive prayers, but they are of no consequence. God answers sincere prayers spoken from the hearts of humble men and women who seek Him secretly.

When Christians pray, they are entering into the holy presence of God. Prayer is an intimate time of close communion and fellowship with their heavenly Father. A relationship with God is developed. Remember, prayer is a two-way communication whereby man speaks his heart to God and, in turn, God speaks to His children through His Word.

8

THE MODEL PRAYER

MATTHEW 6:9-15

This passage of Scripture is universally known as "The Lord's Prayer," but this prayer can be rightly called "The Model Prayer." Another more lengthy prayer is found in John 17 where Jesus prayed to His Father for His disciples and those who would come to know Him through their faithful witness. However, it is this prayer that is widely known as "The Lord's Prayer."

In Israel, near the Sea of Galilee, it is so beautiful for me to sit alone, early in the morning, and watch the sun come up. There I read my Bible, meditate on the Scriptures, pray, and ask God to speak to me. As I have intimate communion with God, the Scriptures just come alive.

Jesus taught His disciples the importance of communion with God in prayer. He prayed sometimes all night long! He waited on the will of His Father. As His followers, how much more do we need to pray? We walk by faith, but we need God's guidance and instruction. Prayer is so important in the life of the believer. It is spending time with God so that He can personally speak to our hearts.

OUR FATHER IN HEAVEN — Matthew 6:9

> "In this manner, therefore pray: Our Father in heaven, hallowed be Your name."

When hearing Jesus pray to the Father, one of His disciples said to Him: *"Lord, teach us to pray"* (Luke 11:1). Within the lives of His disciples, there was a yearning to pray in the same manner they heard Jesus intimately pray to the Father.

Jesus understood their need to express themselves to the Father. He told them, "*When you pray say, 'Our Father in heaven hallowed be Your name.'* " He instructed His disciples to begin their prayers by giving glory and honor to the name of God their Father, who sits on the throne of heaven, before praying for any personal needs. God is holy, and His disciples were to recognize His holy name. God's name was never to be used in vain—ever.

In the Old Testament (Exodus 3), Moses encountered the Lord God at Mount Horeb—the mountain of God where he was called to deliver God's people out of bondage from Egypt. Moses felt completely inadequate. God made Himself known to Moses by the name *Yahweh*, which means *"I Am who I Am."* God would become whatever Moses needed Him to become—the All Becoming One. He would empower Moses to perform the miraculous acts needed to deliver God's children.

God will become whatever a child of God needs. As a Christian, even though you have earthly parents, you have a heavenly Father. When you come before His presence, you are received as a son or daughter: *"I will be a Father to you, and you shall be My sons and daughters, says the* LORD *Almighty"* (2 Corinthians 6:18).

Prayer always begins with relationship. God is your *Abba*, the Aramaic word that refers to God as "Father." It speaks of a close relationship a child has with their "Daddy." As a child of God, your prayers should be directed to Him. He will never fail you or forget you! He created you in your mother's womb:

> *For You formed my inward parts; You covered me in my mother's womb. I will praise You, for I am fearfully and wonderfully made; marvelous are Your works, and that my soul knows very well. My frame was not hidden from You, when I was made in secret, and skillfully wrought in the lowest parts of the earth. Your eyes*

saw my substance, being yet unformed. And in Your book they all were written, the days fashioned for me, when as yet there were none of them. How precious also are Your thoughts to me, O God! How great is the sum of them! If I should count them, they would be more in number than the sand; when I awake, I am still with You.

PSALM 139:13-18

God Knows Everything About You!

Before you start to ask your heavenly Father to help you with your needs, understand, He already knows them! Christians tend to pray selfishly—for their wants. It is good to discern your selfish desires and recognize what God has truly placed on your heart to pray for.

Allow your prayers to be directed by God's Holy Spirit. He will begin to place unselfish necessities on your heart. Then, as you pray for your needs, you will be perfectly in tune with God's will for your life.

YOUR WILL BE DONE — Matthew 6:10

"Your kingdom come. Your will be done on earth as it is in heaven."

At this point in Jesus' sermon, He placed His disciples' focus on praying specifically for God's kingdom to come. They also needed to grasp the importance of God's will to be done on earth as it is in heaven. In other words, events on earth would run according to His perfect will, just as they do in heaven.

As Christians, it is good to have an eternal perspective. This world is not our home. It is important to petition our heavenly Father for His kingdom to come and for His will to be done on earth. Christians in this century are living in perilous times in these last days.

Nothing will prevent God's will from coming to pass. Therefore we need to be in continual prayer. The next prophetic event to happen on God's calendar that we need to be praying about is the Rapture of the Church. The Rapture is the mysterious, prophetic event of God's removal of the Church from the earth:

> *Behold, I tell you a mystery: We shall not all sleep, but we shall all be changed—in a moment, in the twinkling of an eye, at the last trumpet. For the trumpet will sound, and the dead will be raised incorruptible, and we shall be changed.*

> 1 CORINTHIANS 15:51-52

> *For this we say to you by the word of the Lord, that we who are alive and remain until the coming of the Lord will by no means precede those who are asleep* [those who have died]. *For the Lord Himself will descend from heaven with a shout, with the voice of an archangel, and with the trumpet of God. And the dead in Christ will rise first. Then we who are alive and remain shall be caught up* [raptured] *together with them in the clouds to meet the Lord in the air. And thus we shall always be with the Lord.*

> 1 THESSALONIANS 4:15-17

The greatest sign leading to the Rapture of the Church and meeting Jesus in the air is the rebirth of the nation of Israel. The Jewish people were scattered throughout the world. God had judged them and poured out His fury upon them, because they had profaned His Holy name by their idolatry (Ezekiel 36:18-21).

God has promised that Israel would return back to their land: *"For I will take you from among the nations, gather you out of all countries, and bring you into your own land"* (Ezekiel 36:24). Another event that transpires during that time will be the invasion of Israel by the nations from the north (Ezekiel 38-39), setting the timetable for the Great Tribulation period, which is the last seven years of world history. This will be a time of tribulation like the world has never experienced before. This prophetic insight gives us good reason to pray for the tribulation saints to endure and for God's kingdom to be established on earth.

Revelation 6-9 and Revelation 16 describe these horrendous apocalyptic events. All these catastrophic occurrences will take place during the Great Tribulation period on earth, and they will ultimately lead to the Second Coming of Jesus Christ.

Christ having destroyed the kingdoms of the earth (Revelation 17-18), at the Second Coming, is returning back as KING OF KINGS and LORD OF LORDS in fierceness as a warrior to defeat the rulers of the earth, the Antichrist, the false prophet, and the kings of the earth. He will then set up and establish His kingdom on earth for a thousand years (Revelation 19).

Satan is then bound by an angel and cast into the bottomless pit for a thousand years. Meanwhile, the Tribulation saints who were beheaded for the witness of Jesus and the Word of God for not receiving the mark of the beast live and reign for a thousand years as priests of God and of Christ.

After a thousand years, Satan will be released on earth to deceive the peoples from the four corners of the earth. Fire from heaven will devour them, and the devil will be cast into the Lake of Fire where the Antichrist and the false prophet will be, along with death and hell. They will be tormented day and night forever and ever (Revelation 20).

God will create a new heaven and a new earth. He will establish a new, everlasting kingdom with His servants who shall serve Him. They shall see His face, His name shall be on their foreheads, and they shall reign with Him forever and ever (Revelation 21-22:1-5).

In these last days, are you praying for the kingdom of God to come? Do you have an urgency to share the saving Word of Jesus to the lost souls around you? If not, ask the Lord to give that desire to you. Think about it; through your testimony, they too can have entrance into God's kingdom and be in His presence throughout eternity. Are you praying for God's will to be done on earth as it is in heaven?

OUR DAILY BREAD — Matthew 6:11

> "Give us this day our daily bread."

In Christ's Model Prayer, Jesus continued to direct His disciples on the way they should pray to their heavenly Father. The primary lesson taught was relationship. Prayer was to be an intimate time of communion and fellowship with God the Father.

When the disciples recognized and acknowledged God as their Father in their prayers, they entered into His holy presence in an intimate relationship with Him.

As we enter into the presence of a holy God, it is important for us to have a time of preparation to examine our hearts before Him. There is to be a time of confession of sin so that we are in good standing before God, as we petition Him for our daily needs. Jesus was leading and teaching His disciples about prayer in such a beautiful way. I love that!

His followers were then to pray for God's kingdom to come and for God's will to be done, on earth as it is in heaven. Notice, in His prayer, it had taken Jesus a considerable amount of time before He reached the place where His disciples were instructed to petition God for their daily needs—their daily bread.

The Lord is teaching us to pray for our daily provision, not necessarily for a week, a month or a year, but for our *daily* bread. He is able to meet our *daily* needs! Have you ever considered how God provides day by day for the birds?

I remember watching the birds as they came to help themselves to eat freely from my fig tree. As I observed, I became so blessed to see God's provision for them. Just think. If those birds, which are such little creatures, are taken care of by God, then how much more valuable are you than these? (Matthew 10:29-31). You are of more value because you have been created in His image! He provides! So why do you doubt Him? Think of all the miracles God has done in your life—He is faithful. I love the way Jesus ministers to our hearts.

When a person becomes self-confident because they trust in their own resources—investments and money in the bank—there is a real danger that exists. Even though they feel like they do not have to worry, wealth can bring a false security. What if the financial economy of the world suddenly goes bankrupt?

Our entire dependence should be on God! Hudson Taylor, born on May 21, 1832, became a British missionary to China. Having spent 51 years of his life on the mission field, he learned firsthand how to depend on God for everything. He gave to us this wise counsel: "God wants you to have something far better than riches and gold, and that is helpless dependence upon Him."

It is important to pray for our daily needs, whether there is money in the bank or not. As believers, we need to have this right mindset. God is Ruler over the earth, and we must learn to trust Him. As our daily needs are met, our faith will grow in Him. Thank and praise God for all He has provided for you!

THE FREEDOM OF FORGIVENESS — Matthew 6:12

> "And forgive us our debts, as we forgive our debtors."

The Sermon on the Mount did not bring people into a position of condemnation. Jesus brought people into a place of freedom where they learned how to live their lives for Christ. Jesus taught them to forgive—it was a command. Forgiveness was something they might have found hard to do, but as children of God, they had to forgive the offenses committed against them.

Think about forgiveness for a moment. Are you a forgiving person? Do you hold anything in your heart against a person? If you do, confess it to God, and He will cleanse your heart. If you have hurt or have done something against someone, pray for God's perfect timing to tell them you are sorry. He will enable you to forgive. Ask God to give you a love for that person, and He will.

Despite the other person's reaction, God will honor your obedient actions. If you do your part and try to make things right, you can sleep like a baby knowing you have done what was right before God. Forgiveness brings freedom from harbored hate and bitterness.

If you remain in bitterness, it will hurt you and others. Your heart needs to be right before the Lord. Hardheartedness and unforgiveness will cause you not to have peace with God. Some people may say, "You do not understand the situation." It can be extremely difficult to forgive, but let me remind you why you are supposed to forgive other people.

When Jesus forgave you of your sins, they were thrown as far as the east is from the west, and He remembers them no more (Psalm 103:12). All of your past sins are gone. He forgave you—fully and completely. Can you not comprehend that if you have been forgiven by God, then you need to turn around and forgive others? That is what the Bible teaches.

Billy Graham spoke about rebuilding our broken relationships through forgiveness:

> "Forgiveness does not come easily to us, especially when someone we have trusted betrays our trust. And yet if we do not learn to forgive, we will discover that we can never rebuild trust."[4]

How can God bless you and continue to speak to you if you are not willing to obey Him and speak to the person you need to forgive? May God speak to your heart to forgive family members, friends, and even your enemies. We truly need to follow Jesus' example of forgiveness, seen when He was dying on the Cross: *"Father, forgive them; for they know not what they do"* (Luke 23:34, KJV).

DELIVER US FROM THE EVIL ONE — Matthew 6:13

"And do not lead us into temptation, but deliver us from the evil one. For Yours is the kingdom and the power and the glory forever. Amen."

Jesus concluded the Model Prayer by explaining the necessity to pray for deliverance from Satan, because His disciples would face extreme spiritual warfare. It was a reality to face. Their defense was to pray to their Father for deliverance in times of testing and temptation. Who is the evil one? That serpent of old called Satan, the Devil, and the deceiver of the brethren who deceives the whole world—the accuser of the brethren (Revelation 12:9-10).

Satan is your adversary; he is a wicked, spiritual, angelic being. A description of him is found in Ezekiel 28:12-19:

"Son of man, take up a lamentation for the king of Tyre, [a symbolic type of Satan] *and say to him, 'Thus says the Lord GOD: "You were the seal of perfection, full of wisdom and perfect in beauty. You were in Eden, the garden of God; every precious stone was your covering: the sardius, topaz, and diamond, beryl, onyx, and jasper, sapphire, turquoise, and emerald with gold. The workmanship of your timbrels and pipes was prepared for you on the day you were created.*

"You were the anointed cherub who covers; I established you; you were on the holy mountain of God; you walked back and forth in the midst of fiery stones. You were perfect in your ways from the day you were created, till iniquity was found in you.

"By the abundance of your trading you became filled with violence within, and you sinned; therefore I cast you as a profane thing out of the mountain of God; and I destroyed you, O covering cherub, from the midst of the fiery stones.

"Your heart was lifted up because of your beauty; you corrupted your wisdom for the sake of your splendor; I cast you to the ground, I laid you before kings, that they might gaze at you.

"You defiled your sanctuaries by the multitude of your iniquities, by the iniquity of your trading; therefore I brought fire from your midst; it devoured you, and I turned you to ashes upon the earth in the sight of all who saw you. All who knew you among the peoples are astonished at you; You have become a horror, and shall be no more forever." ' "

Satan is always there to tempt you; he comes only to rob, steal and destroy (John 10:10). Only God can deliver us from this fierce, evil one as we go to Him in prayer.

Satan does not want you to be a spiritual Christian, but instead, to remain a carnal person; he preys on those who are surrendered to their fleshly passions and desires. While people sleep, he studies them and plans the next temptation. He deceives people. Satan is the Father of lies (John 8:44). He deceives as many people as he can so they will suffer an eternity in hell—that is his ultimate goal.

The Apostle Peter warns us: *Be sober, be vigilant; because your adversary the devil walks about like a roaring lion, seeking whom he may devour. Resist him, steadfast in the faith…* (1 Peter 5:8-9).

Prior to Jesus beginning His ministry, He was led by the Spirit into the wilderness to be tempted by Satan. Jesus submitted Himself to God and the Holy Spirit. In the wilderness, where nothing grows, Jesus fasted for forty days and forty nights. Satan came and tempted Him, in His weakened condition, twisting the Scriptures, but Jesus used the Word of God to stand against Satan's temptations:

> And when He had fasted forty days and forty nights, afterward He was hungry. Now when the tempter came to Him, he said, "If You are the Son of God, command that these stones become bread." But He answered and said, "It is written, 'Man shall not live by bread alone, but by every word that proceeds from the mouth of God.'" Then the devil took Him up into the holy city, set Him on the pinnacle of the temple, and said to Him, "If You are the Son of God, throw Yourself down. For it is written: 'He shall give His angels charge over you,' and, 'In their hands they shall bear you up, lest you dash your foot against a stone.'" Jesus said to him, "It is written again, 'You shall not tempt the LORD your God.'" Again, the devil took Him up on an exceedingly high mountain, and showed Him all the kingdoms of the world and their glory. And he said to Him, "All these things I will give You if You will fall down and worship me." Then Jesus said to him, "Away with you, Satan! For it is written, 'You shall worship the LORD your God, and Him only you shall serve.'" Then the devil left Him, and behold, angels came and ministered to Him.
>
> MATTHEW 4:2-11

The Word of God and prayer are the Christians' weapons used to defeat Satan. In the Model Prayer, Jesus taught His disciples to pray to the heavenly Father to be delivered from the evil one when facing tough times of temptation. Jesus is our Advocate—Lawyer. He knows exactly what it is like to go through times of extreme temptation, and He will help us.

During periods of temptation, each of us has been given the freedom to make choices. There is always an open door to escape from the temptations we are enduring:

> *No temptation has overtaken you except such as is common to man; but God is faithful, who will not allow you to be tempted beyond what you are able, but with the temptation will also make the way of escape, that you may be able to bear it.*

> 1 CORINTHIANS 10:13

God is faithful! God will deliver us from the tempter and his temptations. Jesus ends His prayer by emphasizing that the kingdom, power and glory belong to God forever. Amen!

CHRIST-LIKE FORGIVENESS — Matthew 6:14-15

"For if you forgive men their trespasses, your heavenly Father will also forgive you. But if you do not forgive men their trespasses, neither will your Father forgive your trespasses."

Jesus continued His sermon once again. He placed great emphasis on the attitude of forgiveness. God knew men's hearts were wicked, and people are generally found to be unpleasant and unforgiving. They easily hold onto grudges against anyone who has wronged them. Yet a child of God needs to obediently practice forgiveness.

Jesus warned people of the terrible consequences to those who were just not willing to forgive the offenses of others. The reason was clear; they would not receive forgiveness for their sins unless they willingly forgave others. When a person chooses to forgive someone, their heavenly Father will forgive them; but if they choose to harbor unforgiveness in their heart instead, then they can expect their heavenly Father not to forgive them—it's just that simple.

If there is unforgiveness in your heart toward a person, God will not forgive you for your trespasses until you make it right in His sight. No matter how many times you come into His presence, you cannot hold on to unforgiveness or resentment in your heart—no possible way!

Understanding the forgiveness of God toward yourself can help you willingly forgive others. Famous Christian author and apologist C.S. Lewis adds these thoughts to help us further understand the biblical concept of forgiveness: "To be a Christian means to forgive the inexcusable because God has forgiven the inexcusable in you." David understood this concept and asked God to forgive him of his sin of adultery, so that he might be forgiven of God: *Wash me thoroughly from my iniquity, and cleanse me from my sin... Create in me a clean heart, O God, and renew a steadfast spirit within me* (Psalm 51:2, 10).

If you do not have forgiveness in your heart for others, then how can your heavenly Father forgive you? Please make sure your heart is right with God, as well as with the person for whom you had harbored unforgiveness.

However, if that person has unforgiveness toward you, and they retain bitterness in their heart, that is not your problem. That is between them and the Lord. Make sure your relationship with God is in good standing.

In your walk with God, forgiveness is an important aspect, because, through forgiveness, God is able to work in the other person's life. You will not have hindered them from entering into the kingdom of God.

Think about what Jesus has said to you personally. Who do you need to forgive today? Have you heeded Jesus' warning? Remember, you can forgive others of their sins on the premise that God has forgiven you of your sins. Christians are to be loving and forgiving. Are you?

9

PRAYER AND FASTING

MATTHEW 6:16-18

During Jesus' ministry, when the Pharisees fasted, they changed their appearance to look very somber and sad. People obviously knew they were fasting. Jesus taught His disciples that these hypocritical Pharisees already had their reward—recognition of men.

A FAÇADE OF FASTING — Matthew 6:16-18

"Moreover, when you fast, do not be like the hypocrites, with a sad countenance. For they disfigure their faces that they may appear to men to be fasting. Assuredly, I say to you, they have their reward. But you, when you fast, anoint your head and wash your face, so that you do not appear to men to be fasting, but to your Father who is in the secret place; and your Father who sees in secret will reward you openly."

Have you ever noticed another believer at church looking very pale, and you approached them to ask inquiringly, "Are you sick?" If they answered slowly and gloomily, "No, I am fasting," do they really just want people to know they are fasting?

I will always remember Pastor Chuck Smith's example of not making a pretense when fasting. Quite often, elderly people could not attend church because of a physical ailment. Chuck would visit them in their homes to fellowship and minister to them. On one occasion, a sweet, little, old lady offered him a piece of cake. Even though Pastor Chuck was fasting, he would go ahead, break his fast, pray, eat the cake, and continue his fast another time—so simple.

True Biblical Fasting

Jesus taught His disciples the correct attitude of true prayer and fasting. They should not purposely draw attention to themselves to be noticed in public. Instead, they should refresh their appearances, anoint their heads with oil, and wash their faces—go about their normal lives.

Fasting was to be understood as a time of self-denial to draw close to the Lord. It should be done in secret, privately before the Lord. Nobody need know His disciples were fasting. As they directed their prayers to God, who dwells in the secret place unseen, He would see them and reward them openly.

Christians need to grasp the full purpose of biblical fasting with the understanding that it is not something believers are required to do; it is not a rule, but a voluntary practice. One of the reasons to fast is for the purpose of consecration—setting apart our lives for God. The discipline of self-denial in fasting will cause a Christian to grow spiritually, to have spiritual power, and to become close to the heart of God. They will know that the hand of God is upon their lives—so important.

When a believer is facing a desperate situation—a very difficult trial—this is another good reason to fast and pray. After a time of prayer and fasting, wait upon God for His answers. Know for certain, He can move in a mighty way in any circumstance. It is God who will receive all the glory for the way He works among us.

King David, the sweet psalmist of Israel, drew close to God when wicked men came against him. While quietly waiting on God, he experienced God's strength, protection and presence. Psalm 27:14 captures his unwavering trust in his God. His confident thoughts encourage us to: *Wait on the LORD; be of good courage, and He shall strengthen your heart; wait, I say, on the LORD!*

Fasting can be used for any specific reason—to set the sinner free, to loose the bonds of wickedness, and to undo heavy burdens placed on themselves or on others. Whatever the reason for your fast, know God's answer can come immediately or sometimes weeks, months or even years. It is important not to become impatient in your prayers. Remember, you are praying according to the will of God—not according to your will.

When you have made the decision to pray and fast, realize this is an intimate time of fellowship between you and God. Find a quiet place where you cannot be disturbed while you pray and wait on the Lord. Pour out your heart before God in sincerity and truth. Make sure to have your Bible with you. God desires to communicate with you through His Word.

Maybe, as a believer, you have never tried fasting. Then pray about it before you attempt to do so. Check with your doctor first before beginning a fast, as it is not for everybody, especially if you have health issues. God will give you strength, wisdom and insight in fasting. I recommend Christians read, *God's Chosen Fast* by Arthur Wallis. He wrote:

> "When we fast, how long we fast, the nature of the fast and the spiritual objectives we have before us are all God's choice, to which the obedient disciple gladly responds."[5]

Denying yourself a meal for any period of time will cause your earthly, bodily appetite for food to increase. About the fourth day, your sense of smell is heightened, and you begin thinking, *Where is that smell coming from?* All you can smell is food! Bacon and eggs! While driving past a hamburger stand, you think, *That smell is so good!* Your sense of smell and hunger makes you crave eating a hamburger! Human bodies crave being fed! Fasting is the denial of this natural desire. Know that as you start to pray and fast, Satan will begin to tempt you in every way possible. Food begins to be so tempting, yet you must deny yourself.

A person can decide on what they want to give up for the Lord. They can choose to fast from all food or certain foods for one, two or three meals—depending on what they can bear. Others fast from social media or time spent watching television. Whatever you choose, do not fast for forty days, or we shall be doing your funeral—for sure!

Remember, there were only three people who fasted forty days and forty nights: Moses, Elijah and Jesus. On these three occasions, the fast was accomplished supernaturally. Moses met with God on Mount Sinai, taking with him two new tablets of stone because Moses, in anger, had cast the first stone tablets down, and they were broken because the people of Israel were worshiping a golden calf (Exodus 32:19; Exodus 34:1). God, once again, wrote the Ten Commandments. During this time, while in the presence of God, Moses neither ate bread nor drank water: *So he was there with the LORD forty days and forty nights; he neither ate bread nor drank water. And He [God] wrote on the tablets the words of the covenant, the Ten Commandments* (Exodus 34:28).

The prophet Elijah fled from Queen Jezebel because she had threatened his life. Elijah was so discouraged that he prayed he might die. While he soundly slept under a broom tree, an angel touched him, woke the prophet, and gave him something to eat and drink. Supernaturally, in the strength of that food, Elijah journeyed for forty days and forty nights without eating. He traveled as far as Horeb, the mountain of God (1 Kings 19:1-8).

Jesus fasted before he began His Galilean ministry. He wanted to be surrendered to God's will, to be empowered for 3½ years of ministry. He did not go in His own strength. Jesus was led by the Spirit into the wilderness where Satan tempted Him: *Then Jesus was led up by the Spirit into the wilderness to be tempted by the devil. And when He had fasted forty days and forty nights, afterward He was hungry* (Matthew 4:1-2).

Jesus had fasted forty days and nights, and since He was 100% God and 100% human, He became hungry. Satan came to tempt Jesus when He was weak. Satan challenged the authority of Christ as Creator, saying: *"If You are the Son of God, command that these stones become bread"* (Matthew 4:3).

The word *if* is actually the word "since." So Satan was actually saying, "Since you are God, you can turn stones into bread." He knew Jesus was God. After Jesus overcame all the devil's temptations by using the Word of God, Satan left Him for a season. The angels then came to minister to Him (Matthew 4:3-11; Luke 4:13). These three examples should be of great encouragement to us because as Moses, Elijah and Jesus fasted, they remained empowered to do God's perfect will.

Fasting for Deliverance

Jesus knew His disciples needed to engage in prayer and fasting as they ministered among the many necessities of the people. There were instances where prayer alone was not enough; it would be necessary to pray and fast.

On one occasion, a desperate man approached Jesus' disciples to heal his son. He was perplexed because his son was demon possessed and greatly tormented. The demons tried to destroy him, even causing him to fall into fire and water, but the disciples could do nothing to heal him. Instead, Jesus had to rebuke the demon (Matthew 17:14-18).

In defeat, the disciples asked Jesus why they could not cast out the demon. Good question! Jesus uncovered the reason and what action was necessary:

> *"Because of your unbelief; for assuredly, I say to you, if you have faith as a mustard seed, you will say to this mountain, 'Move from here to there,' and it will move; and nothing will be impossible for you. However, this kind does not go out except by prayer and fasting."*
>
> MATTHEW 17:20-21

In the past, I have witnessed and prayed for people who were demon possessed. They will often speak in a different voice. Sometimes, while praying, the demon will come out quickly; other times it takes a much longer time. In these demonic situations, anyone not knowing Christ, or a carnal Christian, should not be there. Only those fully committed to Jesus Christ. In the battle, you need spiritual people who are filled with the Holy Spirit.

Fasting and the Ministry

In the Church at Antioch, as Barnabas, Simeon, Lucius, Manaen, and Saul ministered to the Lord and fasted, the Holy Spirit directed them in the work of the ministry: *As they ministered to the Lord and fasted, the Holy Spirit said, "Now separate to Me Barnabas and Saul for the work to which I have called them"* (Acts 13:2).

The leadership of the church laid hands on Barnabas and Saul and sent them away: *Then, having fasted and prayed, and laid hands on them, they sent them away* (Acts 13:3). God had a purpose for their lives:

> *And when they had preached the gospel to that city and made many disciples, they returned to Lystra, Iconium, and Antioch, strengthening the souls of the disciples, exhorting them to continue in the faith, and saying, "We must through many tribulations enter the kingdom of God."*
>
> ACTS 14:21-22

This is very interesting! Fasting happened before Barnabas and Saul were called to a certain work in the ministry. These men were first waiting, praying and fasting before they were separated to the Lord.

If you have the desire to be in the ministry, pray and fast. The Holy Spirit will direct you to the place where you are to be used in the body of Christ. Some Christians are called to be missionaries. As you pray and fast, the Lord will send you where He wants you to go. It is vital to wait on the Lord for His perfect will.

At Calvary Chapel, we pray for those who desire to be in the ministry. We want people who prove themselves in the church over a period of time. There has to be maturity. God shows us different people as we watch them serve and see that they are faithful in the small things. God can give them the opportunity for the greater things (Luke 16:10).

Biblically, it is important for leadership not to lay hands on someone suddenly: *Lay hands suddenly on no man...* (1 Timothy 5:22 KJV). Never anoint and pray for someone to be in ministry who is immature or before their character has been tested. It is best to wait. Too many times, these individuals become a problem to the church and to the Lord.

Religious and Worldly Fasting

Many religions practice prayer and fasting. Traditionally, Buddhist monks do not eat after noon until the dawn of the next day. This type of fasting is called an intermittent fast, thought to teach them self-control. During this time, they give themselves to meditation and chanting. All these practices are empty; it is a futile fast which has no spiritual benefit.

Buddhists used to practice extreme forms of fasting that led to emaciation—malnutrition. Generally, past the fifteenth day is when your body begins to starve and deteriorate, and, if you continue, you are on your way to dying—it is just a matter of time.

Countless people fast to lose weight; this often stems from a worldly desire to look good physically and to perhaps fit better in clothing. All over the world, you will find people who are obsessed with their bodies. They are in love with themselves and make their bodies their god.

Sometimes women feel insecure about themselves. They make it their aim to fast to try and stay skinny for their husbands—to satisfy them. Both men and women worry about their bodies. They spend a great deal of time trying to maintain a nice body to the extent of actually making themselves sick. What people often forget is that our human bodies naturally age—weaken. This temporal body becomes in need of repair. Honestly, why can we not just be normal and be content with ourselves?

God's Chosen Fast and Its Rewards

God told the prophet Isaiah to go tell His people the transgressions they had committed. As they fasted, eagerly seeking God in the temple in a pretense of obeying His ordinances, they wondered why God had not answered their prayers: " *'Why have we fasted,' they say, 'and You have not seen? Why have we afflicted our souls, and You take no notice?'* " (Isaiah 58:3).

God knew their worship was just an outward show. Their hearts were far from Him, so they received no answer. Isaiah revealed to them their wicked hearts:

> *"In fact, in the day of your fast you find pleasure, and exploit all your laborers. Indeed you fast for strife and debate, and to strike with the fist of wickedness. You will not fast as you do this day, to make your voice heard on high. Is it a fast that I have chosen, a day for a man to afflict his soul? Is it to bow down his head like a bulrush, and to spread out sackcloth and ashes? Would you call this a fast, and an acceptable day to the LORD?"*

ISAIAH 58:3-5

God's chosen fast would please the heart of God:

> *"Is this not the fast that I have chosen: to loose the bonds of wickedness, to undo the heavy burdens, to let the oppressed go free, and that you break every yoke? Is it not to share your bread with the hungry, and that you bring to your house the poor who are cast out; when you see the naked, that you cover him, and not hide yourself from your own flesh?"*

ISAIAH 58:6-7

Isaiah the prophet went on to say, when fasting was done with the right heart attitude and for the right reason, great spiritual rewards were given. God openly rewards those who engage in strenuous, victorious, spiritual warfare through fasting:

> *"Then your light shall break forth like the morning, your healing shall spring forth speedily, and your righteousness shall go before you; the glory of the LORD shall be your rear guard. Then you shall call, and the LORD will answer; you shall cry, and He will say, 'Here I am.' If you take away the yoke from your midst, the pointing of the finger, and speaking wickedness, if you extend your soul to the hungry and satisfy the afflicted soul, then your light shall dawn in the darkness, and your darkness shall be as the noonday.*

> *"The LORD will guide you continually, and satisfy your soul in drought, and strengthen your bones; you shall be like a watered garden, and like a spring of water, whose waters do not fail. Those from among you shall build the old waste places; you shall raise up the foundations of many generations; and you shall be called the Repairer of the Breach, the Restorer of Streets to Dwell In."*

> ISAIAH 58:8-12

Satan, our archenemy, does not want Christians to fast because their intuitive knowledge of God and their senses will be spiritually sharpened. Christians will be enabled to become more in tune with the Holy Spirit. They will be given spiritual gifts, such as a word of wisdom or a word of knowledge (1 Corinthians 12:7-8).

A word of wisdom is the divine ability to speak wisdom for a difficult situation or when an important decision needs to be made. It is done very naturally, and often this spiritual gift is used without even being noticed. A word of knowledge gives a person the supernatural ability to know something they would not have otherwise known. The Spirit of God has revealed it to them. Both of these spiritual gifts will help believers discern God's voice.

Remember, in your giving to others, servanthood, praying, and fasting, it is all about your heart attitude—doing things unto the Lord. We are to be on target with Him. Another quote by Arthur Wallis gives credence to an acceptable fast before the Lord:

> God reminds His people that the acceptable fast is the one which He has chosen. Fasting, like prayer, must be God-initiated and God-ordained if it is to be effective.[6]

Once a year, the entire nation of Israel would fast on the Day of Atonement, one of the holiest days of the year. Fasting was something the Jews were accustomed to doing. Throughout Israel's history, the nation was called upon to fast and seek God's face in humble repentance, asking Him for His deliverance. God exhorted His people:

> *...if My people who are called by My name will humble themselves, and pray and seek My face, and turn from their wicked ways, then I will hear from heaven, and will forgive their sin and heal their land.*

> 2 CHRONICLES 7:14

How has this chapter changed your view toward prayer and fasting? Will you add this Christian discipline to your daily life? Will you humble yourself before God and fast for America, so our nation can experience a new revival?

10

ETERNAL PERSPECTIVE

MATTHEW 6:19-24

After Jesus spoke about communion with God, prayer, and fasting—which is self-denial, He turned to the subject of material gain. Jesus wanted the people to have an eternal perspective toward their possessions. There is an enormous benefit of laying up true treasures in heaven. They will never be moth-eaten, rust cannot tarnish them, and thieves cannot steal heavenly treasures.

WHERE IS YOUR TREASURE? — Matthew 6:19-21

"Do not lay up for yourselves treasures on earth, where moth and rust destroy and where thieves break in and steal; but lay up for yourselves treasures in heaven, where neither moth nor rust destroys and where thieves do not break in and steal. For where your treasure is, there your heart will be also."

There is nothing wrong with possessions, but if they begin to possess you, then they become a problem. Do not allow yourself to be controlled by material gain. It cannot rule and dominate over your life, because then you are not free to serve the Lord.

Think about this concept for a second. Everyone has a god—it can be your job, your car, or your Harley-Davidson. It can even be a person—your wife or a child. Where are your deepest affections? If God is not first, then something else is your god. Where do you place your life's focus? That is your treasure, and that is where your heart is! Whatever or whoever has taken possession of your life, other than Sovereign God Almighty, is an idol that is governing over you and will ultimately destroy you.

Do you really know what your first love is in life? If you love that possession or person more than you love God, you are in trouble. There is a weakness in your life. Be on guard because you are not to be governed by anything other than Christ.

Take a true test of your heart. What would happen if your earthly treasures were taken from you? Would you feel your life is finished? Our earthly treasures can be swept away in seconds by a flood, destroyed by an earthquake, or annihilated by a tornado or a worldwide pandemic.

In the face of sudden trials, will your faith be destroyed, or will your faith in God maintain you? Billy Graham, the world-renowned evangelist, had an eternal perspective in his life. He left us with this soul-searching question to answer:

> "Can people tell from the emphasis we attach to material things whether we have set our affection on things above, or whether we are primarily attached to this world?"[7]

Remember, as a Christian, you are always to look to the eternal, not the temporal. Paul the Apostle encouraged the believer to:

> *Set your mind on things above, not on things on the earth. For you died, and your life is hidden with Christ in God. When Christ who is our life appears, then you also will appear with Him in glory.*

> COLOSSIANS 3:2-4

With an eternal perspective, you can be a good steward of all the things God has given to you. There is nothing wrong with investing in the stock market, but it is volatile; you can lose or gain money. However, if you place your confidence in money, instead of God's provision for you, then how can you really come to fully trust in God? If you are fully trusting in God for your provisions and investing into the work of the Lord, you are laying up for yourselves treasures in heaven—they will always be there; you are never going to lose them.

It is good to evaluate where you are keeping your treasures. Where are your treasures? Do you have them stored away on this earth or in heaven? Are you living with eternity in view?

Keep in mind that any temporal things you store away can become moth eaten or stolen by thieves; they are temporal—not eternal. When you die, you cannot take any of your treasures with you. They are left behind for someone else to enjoy. It is important to make sure you use wisdom when leaving behind any of your earthly possessions. Those who inherit your wealth might spend it unwisely and destroy their lives—be careful!

THE LAMP OF THE BODY — Matthew 6:22-23

> "The lamp of the body is the eye. If therefore your eye is good, your whole body will be full of light. But if your eye is bad, your whole body will be full of darkness. If therefore the light that is in you is darkness, how great is that darkness!"

Jesus warned His disciples to keep guard over their eyes. If they guarded their eyes from impure things, they would protect their souls. The eye is the entrance to the soul. Those who belong to Christ need to be careful about the things they allow into their lives through the entrance of their eyes.

Christians, be watchful about what you permit your eyes to see, this will keep your life pure. Lustful images in magazines are appealing; these pictures will catch a person's eyes and bring them to a place of bondage. People enticed by lustful images will not be satisfied with only looking at these images; they will want more and more. Lust always leads to sin:

> Let no one say when he is tempted, "I am tempted by God"; for God cannot be tempted by evil, nor does He Himself tempt anyone. But each one is tempted when he is drawn away by his own desires and enticed. Then, when desire has conceived, it gives birth to sin; and sin, when it is full-grown, brings forth death.
>
> JAMES 1:13-15

The nature of the heart is evil, and evil can possess you if you allow it: "*The heart is deceitful above all things, and desperately wicked; who can know it?*" (Jeremiah 17:9). Think of how many young people have been destroyed by looking at filthy images and movies. In our society, people flip through television channels and social media to view lewd programs. Even the commercials are sexually appealing. Sex sells. If you go into Hollywood, your heart will be broken because you will see how many young men and women have been seduced into prostitution—it is sad. How great is that darkness!

Radio stations play music that appeal to a person's flesh—carnal desires. Protect your ears and keep your mind pure! Do not become addicted to listening to sinful things; it will draw you down a path of destruction. Think about the way you are influencing your family—spouse, children and friends. Do you want them to follow your example? Those watching you will be influenced by the way you live. Will they follow the light or be lost in great darkness?

WHO WILL YOU SERVE? — Matthew 6:24

> "No one can serve two masters; for either he will hate the one and love the other, or else he will be loyal to the one and despise the other. You cannot serve God and mammon."

Jesus continued to press the point about material gain. He shared with those who gathered to hear Him that they could not serve God and wealth—*two masters*. There is no middle ground. Either God is number one, or people are being controlled by their possessions.

This can also apply to those who have made another person first in their lives. In the late seventies, an incorrect teaching began to circulate in the churches. Instead of placing God first, people began to miss church on Sundays and participate in secular activities. Christian couples were taught to neglect their church and family in order to spend time alone as a couple. They believed it was healthy spiritually for their marriage. Families walked away from Church because of this erroneous teaching.

Serving the Lord should be a family priority. God must be first, and then everything else will flow together. As you look at your priorities, are they in harmony with what Jesus taught? *"But seek first the kingdom of God and His righteousness, and all these things shall be added to you"* (Matthew 6:33).

The Rich Young Ruler

The story of the Rich Young Ruler is told in Matthew 19:16-22. It is also found in Mark 10:17-31, and again in Luke18:18-30, but with other details. It is thought that this young man was a wealthy ruler of a synagogue. As Jesus encountered the rich young ruler, He pointed him toward the riches of salvation.

This wealthy young man came to Jesus with such excitement, a lot of confidence, and the right attitude. He had recognized there was something different about Jesus; this Teacher was not like the Pharisees and Sadducees. In all sincerity, he asked Jesus some very good questions. Listen to the beginning conversation between them in Matthew 19:16: *Now behold, one came and said to Him* [Jesus], *"Good Teacher, what good thing shall I do that I may have eternal life?"*

This is one of the greatest questions in life for all of us to consider. People will often ask, "What does it take to get into the kingdom of God? What do I have to do?" Like the rich young ruler, the majority of people immediately think of works: "What good things shall I do? Do I have to join the church? Make a commitment to give money to the church? Perhaps I need to do good deeds, like helping an old person across the road. Will any of these things help me gain entrance into the kingdom?" There is no way a person can pay their way into the kingdom of God. No amount of money can buy salvation, nor will the sacrificial acts of kindness a person does for God gain them entrance into the kingdom of God—period.

Understand, in this world there are a lot of people who need Christ, but, like the rich young ruler, these people are mistaken if they think they are going to heaven because of their good works—they are not. Salvation is not about works; it is about faith. A person must believe that if they truly come to God in repentance for their sins, then He will accept them. God will forgive them of all their sins—past, present and future. Salvation is a free gift, and it is available for each one of us: *For the wages of sin is death, but the gift of God is eternal life in Christ Jesus our Lord* (Romans 6:23).

Jesus responded to the young man with another good question: *So He* [Jesus] *said to him, "Why do you call Me good? No one is good but One, that is, God. But if you want to enter into life, keep the commandments"* (Matthew 19:17).

There are Ten Commandments: the first four Commandments speak of our relationship to God; the following six Commandments deal with our human nature. We are all guilty of breaking the Commandments. If you answer, "No, I have not," then I would have to say to you, "You are lying," because every one of us has broken them. We break them every single day.

There are people who have deep within their conscience and heart the belief that they are good. They are not drug addicts or alcoholics, but they live uprightly, doing good deeds. They believe they are on the way to heaven. Yet we all have sinned, and the Word of God tells us sin separates a person from God: *But your iniquities have separated you from your God; and your sins have hidden His face from you, so that He will not hear* (Isaiah 59:2). The Scriptures also plainly state:

> *As it is written: "There is none righteous, no, not one; there is none who understands; there is none who seeks after God. They have all turned aside; they have together become unprofitable; there is none who does good, no, not one."*

ROMANS 3:10-12

Only God is good. Trying to keep the Ten Commandments should have shown the rich young ruler that he was a sinner in need of a Savior. The young man needed to see he was not perfect. Yet confidently, the rich young ruler asked: *"Which ones?"* Jesus replied:

> *" 'You shall not murder,' 'You shall not commit adultery,' 'You shall not steal,' 'You shall not bear false witness,' 'Honor your father and your mother,' and, 'You shall love your neighbor as yourself. ' " The young man said to Him, "All these things I have kept from my youth."*

MATTHEW 19:18-20

The rich young ruler seemed excited; he was narrowing down what he thought to be the way to eternal life. He had kept the commandments Jesus mentioned from his youth. The young man decided to ask the Teacher one more final question:

> *"What do I still lack?" Jesus said to him, "If you want to be perfect, go, sell what you have and give to the poor, and you will have treasure in heaven; and come, follow Me."*

MATTHEW 19:20-21

If the rich young ruler wanted to be *perfect*, meaning "mature or complete," he was to sell everything and give it to the poor. Then he would have treasures in heaven. Jesus called the rich young ruler to follow Him, and in doing so, Jesus tested his heart to see what he loved more—God or his possessions.

What was the young man's tragic response? *But when the young man heard that saying, he went away sorrowful, for he had great possessions* (Matthew 19:22). This young man was very rich; he had everything he needed in life. Sadly, he had anchored himself to his worldly riches, and sorrowfully, the young man turned away from following Jesus. His heart was revealed.

What a disappointing response! Yet if this man had made a commitment to sell everything and follow Christ, Jesus would have seen the genuineness of his heart, and probably the young ruler would not have had to sell his riches.

Let me ask you this personal question, "Is Jesus your Master?" You cannot serve two masters. "What is Jesus asking you to leave behind so that you can follow Him?" Will you leave sorrowful like the rich young ruler, or will you follow Jesus with a joyful heart? When you choose to follow Jesus, He will become your first priority, and your life will be used to bring glory and honor to Him.

If you obey the call to pursue Jesus, then you will have a life-long passion for doing His will instead of having a passion for your possessions. I have found there are many rich people who are very generous in giving. However, there are others who hoard their riches for themselves; they become very tight with their money.

Think about the people who work in the corporate world. Work can become more important to them than anything else! They work late every night—all week long. Their main focus is, "I am going to make another million!" Yet they are never satisfied with the next million. How many people strive to earn more and more, but under the constant stress, suffer a major heart attack?

People need to learn to be content and happy with whatever God gives them; otherwise, they will begin to covet other people's possessions— cars or houses. When a person is content, they can be used greatly in the kingdom of God. When God tests their heart, He sees a genuine, giving heart, not a covetous heart.

After the disciples witnessed the rich young ruler's dejected response, Jesus turned to His disciples and said:

> *"Assuredly, I say to you that it is hard for a rich man to enter the kingdom of heaven. And again I say to you, it is easier for a camel to go through the eye of a needle than for a rich man to enter the kingdom of God."*

> MATTHEW 19:23-24

Jesus stipulated the impossibility of salvation. Whether rich or poor, salvation is given by the grace of God through faith in Jesus—it is a gift from God. Think of your own salvation. How did you come to know the Lord Jesus Christ? What kind of life did you have beforehand? Were you at the end of your rope? How many of us got on our knees before God to ask for His forgiveness, and by God's grace, were freely given the gift of salvation? God just gives it! Now notice the disciple's reaction to Jesus' statement:

> *When His disciples heard it, they were greatly astonished, saying, "Who then can be saved?" But Jesus looked at them and said to them, "With men this is impossible, but with God all things are possible."*

> MATTHEW 19:25-26

With men salvation is impossible, but with God all things are possible. As the rich young ruler was thought to be a wealthy owner of a synagogue, he would have known religion; but what was lacking in his life was a personal relationship with God. He was not born again, and like many sincere, good people, he was merely a religious person, but he needed Christ.

This is what is lacking in so many people's lives today—an intimate relationship with Jesus. People are still trying to be saved by good works. A person needs to come to the Cross and repent of their sins. Then a miracle takes place. They experience a new birth and become saved (John 3).

You see, with God all things, including our salvation, are possible—so important. Religion will lead a person to hell, but a personal love relationship that can only come through Jesus Christ will lead us to heaven.

Then Peter answered Jesus and said, "*See, we have left all and followed You. Therefore, what shall we have?*"

> *So Jesus said to them* [all the disciples], "*Assuredly I say to you, that in the regeneration, when the Son of Man sits on the throne of His glory, you who have followed Me will also sit on twelve thrones, judging the twelve tribes of Israel.*"

MATTHEW 19:28

When Jesus uses the word *assuredly*, it is important to pay close attention to His words. Jesus spoke of the surety of future rewards in His eternal kingdom. Another reference in Luke 22:28-29 also refers to rewards given in His eternal kingdom:

> "*But you are those who have continued with Me in My trials. And I bestow upon you a kingdom, just as My Father bestowed one upon Me, that you may eat and drink at My table in My kingdom, and sit on thrones judging the twelve tribes of Israel.*"

Jesus also told His disciples of the rewards gained in this life:

> "*Assuredly, I say to you, there is no one who has left house or brothers or sisters or father or mother or wife or children or lands, for My sake and the gospel's, who shall not receive a hundredfold now in this time—houses and brothers and sisters and mothers and children and lands, with persecutions—and in the age to come, eternal life.*"

MARK 10:29-30

In the light of these heavenly riches, consider the rich young ruler now. If the young man had sold his earthly riches, given them to the poor, and followed Jesus, he would have inherited more than he could have ever imagined! He would have received blessings on earth and the riches of eternal life.

The rich young ruler could not leave his earthly riches to follow Christ; he could not serve two masters. As Christ said— "*You cannot serve God and mammon*" (Matthew 6:24).

The Cost of Discipleship

On another occasion, Jesus taught that in order to follow Him and become His disciple, a person must count the cost:

> *When He* [Jesus] *had called the people to Himself, with His disciples also, He said to them, "Whoever desires to come after Me, let him deny himself, and take up his cross, and follow Me. For whoever desires to save his life will lose it, but whoever loses his life for My sake and the gospel's will save it. For what will it profit a man if he gains the whole world, and loses his own soul? Or what will a man give in exchange for his soul?"*

> MARK 8:34-37

This was the case with the rich young ruler:

> *Then Jesus, looking at him, loved him, and said to him, "...Go your way, sell whatever you have and give to the poor, and you will have treasure in heaven; and come, take up the cross, and follow Me."*

> MARK 10:21

Jesus explained to His disciples the cost of following Him—discipleship. He gave them a call to follow Him, but they would need to forsake everything. In two words, what is the cost of discipleship? Deny all. The way of self-denial is death to self; it is the beginning of an abundant life in Christ. To *deny oneself*, means to "forget about yourself." A self-serving attitude is not worthy of Christ's kingdom. Followers of Christ must love Christ! They must be willing to deny themselves, take up the Cross—the instrument of death to self—and follow Jesus.

Jesus recruits a person to follow the way of the Cross. When you pick up your cross, there has to be a total commitment. There are conditions. His followers must tread the way of suffering in this life in order to enjoy the future life to come. Following Jesus is not a bed of roses, as even roses have thorns that will pierce. You may be hated, rejected, mocked and cruelly persecuted. Are you willing to make the choice to pick up your cross and follow Him? Will you give your life to Jesus?

When it comes down to self-denial and living a life for Christ, many people will fail to do it! Some will deny the Lord in order to indulge in a sinful self-life that has no eternal value, and they will forfeit their eternal salvation. People have to make a determined choice in their minds. Who are they going to serve? You cannot serve two masters— you love the one, and you hate the other. Again, what did Jesus say? *"For what will it profit a man if he gains the whole world, and loses his own soul? Or what will a man give in exchange for his soul?"*

Discipleship will cost you your life! The Cross of Christ is the instrument of death; it is the key to Christian discipleship. A Christian needs to have a life centered in Christ—a disciplined life that is always looking toward the Cross. Yet how many people are selling their souls in this life for money, power or different types of gods they serve and worship?

The classic book titled *The Cost of Discipleship* was written by a German pastor, Dietrich Bonhoeffer. The title of his book was inspired by Jesus' words from Matthew 16:24-25. When World War II broke out in Europe, he fled Germany and came to New York City. The Holy Spirit convicted Bonhoeffer, and he willingly went back to Germany.

He went underground, speaking with the pastors who were giving in to the philosophy of Nazism.

Finally, Bonhoeffer was arrested and imprisoned. While in prison, he wrote many letters called *Dietrich Bonheoffer Letters and Papers from Prison*. His final words were: "This is the end—for me the beginning of life."[8] On April 9, 1945, he was taken to Flossenburg concentration camp and executed—hung by the neck. Bonhoeffer was martyred. He knew the sacrificial life and cost of discipleship. He gave his life for Christ.

When Jesus taught the way of the Cross to His twelve disciples, He said to them: "*And he who does not take his cross and follow after Me is not worthy of Me. He who finds his life will lose it, and he who loses his life for My sake will find it*" (Matthew 10:38-39). These are the words of Jesus. He calls people to come to a place of utter surrender. Those who come to Him, with self-renouncing faith, experience an abundant life and receive eternal life. They live by what Christ has established, the model He set down for them to follow—the crucified life.

A Soul Required

Then He [Jesus] spoke a parable to them, saying: "The ground of a certain rich man yielded plentifully. And he thought within himself, saying, 'What shall I do, since I have no room to store my crops?' So he said, 'I will do this: I will pull down my barns and build greater, and there I will store all my crops and my goods. And I will say to my soul, "Soul, you have many goods laid up for many years; take your ease; eat, drink, and be merry."' But God said to him, 'Fool! This night your soul will be required of you; then whose will those things be which you have provided?' So is he who lays up treasure for himself, and is not rich toward God."

LUKE 12:16-21

In this story, the Parable of the Rich Fool, Jesus dealt with the sin of covetousness, greed, and the need to have an eternal perspective. Notice how the rich man used the word "I" six times and "my" five times. He lived to please himself. As a wealthy man, he was set for life, yet he was not satisfied.

The rich fool decided to build and expand. He thought about his building project and prepared to purchase what he needed, but the voice of God was heard: " *'Fool! This night your soul will be required of you....'* " The wealthy man mistakenly thought he had many years left to enjoy his early retirement and all his possessions—but that very evening he died.

It is not the one who holds the gold that wins! It is the person who is sowing into the kingdom of God. In the end, they will reap great eternal dividends. Many people do not live with the thought that they are going to die, so they do not prepare for eternity when they will stand before the presence of God—sad.

In this life, people have a tendency to accumulate wealth; they strive to have what someone else possesses. The soul never becomes satisfied with possessions. Money does not guarantee happiness or peace. In fact, there are very few people who can handle money and power without being destroyed by them. It is all right to have wealth, but it cannot possess you.

I believe the reason why many people do not come to accept the Gospel is because they persistently pursued so many sparkling gold, diamond, and material things in this life. Yet as people covet these earthly treasures that attract them, they will find in the end, they have become worthless—they are of no eternal value. You cannot take your riches with you!

Christians need to trust in the Lord, not their riches. We should be satisfied with all God has blessed us. Christians should be kind and giving. If God has blessed you with wealth, consider this: you cannot outgive Him.

It is good to remember who has made you wealthy—God! Do not forget. He has given you everything in life.

Job had the right perspective toward life: *And he said: "Naked I came from my mother's womb, and naked shall I return there. The* LORD *gave, and the* LORD *has taken away; blessed be the name of the* LORD*"* (Job 1:21).

Examine your life; do you have an eternal perspective? Are you building your own kingdom or the kingdom of God?

11

ARE YOU WORRIED ABOUT LIFE?

MATTHEW 6:25-34

After Jesus taught His disciples to have an eternal perspective, He was able to make this perfect summation clear to them—they need not worry about their lives.

DO NOT WORRY — Matthew 6:25

"Therefore I say to you, do not worry about your life, what you will eat or what you will drink; nor about your body, what you will put on. Is not life more than food and the body more than clothing?"

In the KJV Bible, Jesus' words are written: *take no thought for your life.* The phrase means "not to be anxious or overly concerned about things." Notice how beautiful this is. In the knowledge of eternity, Jesus' disciples were not to worry about any earthly necessities of life—food, drink or clothing.

Yet people constantly worry. Why is it that we worry so much? No doubt, the reason is people are seeing all the serious problems happening all over the world: fires, floods, earthquakes, hurricanes and pandemics. Many countries remain at war, in constant turmoil, violence and unrest, while others are under constant threat of war. The world seems to be spiraling out of control! Those who frequently listen to the news find these developments frightening—worrisome.

The growing concern in society has caused people's hearts to experience great anxiety. People are fearful about the future—it is scary. Most individuals want to find an escape from their anxieties. Some have developed great dependencies—drinking alcohol or taking drugs—in an attempt to escape their worries. Whatever people try to use to find comfort and hope will create instability. These addictions will only place them into a deeper pit because, in the end, they still have to live in this world and face their problems.

In fact, the future generations seem to have no sense of stability, no sense of integrity, and no sense of direction. In our schools, children are facing intense peer pressure. So many young people have been destroyed through drugs, alcohol, sexual immorality, identity confusion and suicide. Many do not believe in God, and they have become atheistic. As they do not know God, they have no hope. Our youth need our prayerful intercession. It will take the preaching of the Gospel and God's wisdom to reach them. I believe with all my heart, the times we are living in today are like the days of Noah. In these last days, it will take a supernatural work of God to save people in this world.

The reality of what is happening on earth has caused people to lack faith in God. Christians are having their faith tested because there is no guarantee and no security in this world. In Luke 18:1, Jesus encouraged His followers to pray and to not lose heart. Jesus also spoke of His return, His Second Coming, and He said to them: "...when the Son of Man comes, will He really find faith on the earth?" (Luke 18:8)

While living on this earth, Christians need to have faith. People lack faith, but faith is the key factor to help us stop our incessant worrying. Jesus spoke about a faith that has complete confidence in Him—our Provider. God is Jehovah-jireh; this name means "the Lord will provide." Everything we need comes from God. I believe we are living in a time when Christians will need to be on their knees more than ever, praying not only for provision, but for comfort, asking God to reassure them.

It is important to pray for those who do not know Christ, as they will need God's saving grace before they can develop a dependency on Christ through His Word. Christians have a blessed hope through the darkness and perplexing anxieties of this world because they have an intimate relationship with Christ. They remain steadfast, *looking for the blessed hope and glorious appearing of our great God and Savior Jesus Christ* (Titus 2:13).

LOOK AT THE BIRDS — Matthew 6:26-27

"Look at the birds of the air, for they neither sow nor reap nor gather into barns; yet your heavenly Father feeds them. Are you not of more value than they? Which of you by worrying can add one cubit to his stature?"

Jesus focused His audience on their heavenly Father's divine capabilities. He used common sense questions to cause people to think realistically and to rescue them from unnecessary worry. He reasoned with them by saying, "If God feeds the birds, will He not take care of you? Are you not of more value than the birds of the air?" Jesus knew needless worry would plague and enslave people. He lovingly reassured them of God's love and divine care. Their heavenly Father was more than able to supply all their needs.

Christians, like most people, tend to worry, especially when they lack money or material stability. They may panic, thinking, *I do not own a house or have good job security. What am I going to do? I am going to be turning 65, and everything I try to buy will be at a much higher price than I can afford.*

Seriously, when did you grow eighteen inches during the night because of your worrying? The word *stature* means "height, quality, status gained by growth, or age." When you pray to the Lord, realize He is the only One who can help you. Be dependent fully on Him. Even if the economy collapses, the Lord will take care of you. Do not worry! Has God ever failed you yet? When was the last time that God did not meet your needs?

Worrying is senseless—it is unbelief. God does not approve of unbelief because, in actuality, it is questioning Him! Many people get angry with God and blame Him for their situations. Yet the problem is them! They are not trusting in Him for their provision. It is foolish not to trust in the Lord. It is even more foolish to have a life of unbelief. The fate of unbelief will bring you nothing but grief. It will cause you never to trust in Jesus Christ.

Think about it. If God takes care of the sparrows, how much more will He take care of each of us individually? Yet people continue to worry about everything in life. Those who worry teach their children and others around them to worry. Honestly, when we go to bed at night, do we have to worry about breathing? No! Do we not trust God and believe that He is in control of our lives? Then quit worrying.

Consider the negative effects of unnecessary worry. People who suffer from extreme anxiety and worry can hurt their physical and emotional health. Worrying leads you to doubt God's provision and protection over you. Christians need to believe the Word of God, and then they will be able to rest in Him. God can give believers peace that surpasses all understanding. Underline and memorize these verses in Philippians 4:6-7, to combat anxiety:

> Be anxious for nothing, but in everything by prayer and supplication, with thanksgiving, let your requests be made known to God; and the peace of God, which surpasses all understanding, will guard your hearts and minds through Christ Jesus.

I believe the root problem with worry is that some people have not taken the time to read the Bible and get to know the character and attributes of God. How can you know a person without reading their autobiography? You cannot. When reading an autobiography, it is important to capture that person's personality and character. That is why the Word of God is so important. It captures the character and attributes of Jesus Christ. You can know for certain who Jesus is through the study of His two natures, both the humanity and divinity of Christ.

Oswald Chambers was the son of a Baptist preacher in Aberdeen, Scotland. He was born on July 24, 1874, and grew to become an evangelist and teacher. Interestingly, Oswald Chambers was converted under the preaching of Charles Spurgeon.

Oswald Chambers was also a well-known author. He wrote the classic, devotional book, *My Utmost for His Highest*. It remains a beautiful devotional penned for Christians who desire to fully surrender themselves to God. Chambers stated that, "worry is an indication that we think God cannot look after us." He also said: "Faith is deliberate confidence in the character of God whose ways you may not understand at the time."

When a believer grows spiritually, with surety, they know God will take care of them, one step at a time. You see, in the future, every one of us will go through trials, suffering and tragedy. It will come, but if we have the right concept of God, we shall be able to handle those difficulties when they arise.

SO WHY WORRY? — Matthew 6:28-30

> "So why do you worry about clothing? Consider the lilies of the field, how they grow: they neither toil nor spin; and yet I say to you that even Solomon in all his glory was not arrayed like one of these. Now if God so clothes the grass of the field, which today is, and tomorrow is thrown into the oven, will He not much more clothe you, O you of little faith?"

Jesus calmed human anxieties and worries. He continued to ask, *"So why do you worry about clothing?"* Can you answer this question for yourself? Jesus directs anxious souls, those who have a tendency to worry, to have faith in God, as they look upon His creative power—considering the lilies of the field!

As Jesus spoke, the people listening would have been able to look at the beautiful lilies in the valleys and on the hillsides in Israel. Our Creator takes care of all the flowers and grass in the fields. If God can bring the rain and wind, taking care of nature, then He is quite able to take care of each one of us.

Honestly, it is in our very nature to worry about everything in life. People even worry about unnecessary things. We all say, "I want" and "I need." Women worry about having a dress for an event, and men worry about their clothing, too! Yet most of us have a whole closet full of clothing!

Notice, Jesus pinpoints the cause of why we worry—it is our lack of faith, *"...O you of little faith?"* Jesus' questions are so relevant for all of us because we are all inclined to worry. When the rent is due on the first of the month, and the funds for the payment are not available, we fret. God knows the rent money is needed; He knows everything about our situation. Trust in God. Billy Graham gives to us the prescription for ending our worry: "The cure to worry is trust — trust in God, and trust in his love and protection."

GOD KNOWS YOUR NEEDS — Matthew 6:31-32

> "Therefore do not worry, saying, 'What shall we eat?' or 'What shall we drink?' or 'What shall we wear?' For after all these things the Gentiles seek. For your heavenly Father knows that you need all these things."

Jesus continued to address the subject of anxiousness because people indelibly worry! Once again, Jesus reassured all those listening to

Him how unnecessary it was for them to worry. He directed them to their heavenly Father's omniscience—His infinite knowledge of everything. God already knows your needs, and He is able to supply them, so why worry?

God proclaimed this truth about Himself: *"For every beast of the forest is Mine, and the cattle on a thousand hills. I know all the birds of the mountains, and the wild beasts of the field are Mine"* (Psalm 50:10-11). Knowing this, are your worries about shelter, food and water calmed? Our great God Almighty, *El Shaddai*, is "all-sufficient." He is able to sustain all living things. Our heavenly Father will take care of every situation. He provides. We do not have to worry. Be encouraged and comforted by Jesus' message, and trust in the Lord to take care of you—fully and completely.

However, even though God does provide for us, as believers, we should be good stewards of all He has provided. Christians need to be careful with their health and smart with their finances. Each individual needs to take care of their own responsibilities. In the world, we are entrusted with certain duties. God has given to every person spiritual gifts and charges. Christians have been given the charge of stewardship over all God has blessed them with.

Do not be neglectful, but be prepared for life. We have a Christian duty to be responsible. Believers need to seek God's wisdom in finding a job so they can afford a place to live. In life, we need to work hard to provide for all our daily needs. The trouble with some people is that they are lazy, shiftless and thoughtless, and they have a bad attitude. They really do not care about their future. If they find themselves in need, it is not God's fault—it is solely theirs.

SEEK FIRST GOD'S KINGDOM — Matthew 6:33-34

"But seek first the kingdom of God and His righteousness, and all these things shall be added to you. Therefore do not worry about tomorrow, for tomorrow will worry about its own things. Sufficient for the day is its own trouble."

Jesus wisely counseled His followers to have one main focus in life "...*seek first the kingdom of God and His righteousness.*" Christians are to seek first the things that relate to God, in other words, progressing His kingdom on earth—the things that relate to His sovereign will and purposes. Jesus is our King, and we need to be about our King's business.

How is this done? Our relationship with God is of utmost importance because, as we place Him first by spending time with Him in prayer and in our personal devotional time with Him, He will faithfully lead and reveal to us the work we need to do for His kingdom.

Every day, we are to love God first! As Christians, seeking God and His kingdom is to be our first priority. Our entire life pursuit is to seek first the kingdom of God. It is the key to everything we do in life. We always come to God by faith, seeking Him first, and then He will add everything else to us effortlessly without us having to be anxious. Everything will unfold according to His plan and His will.

The word *seek* means "to go after, to strive, to pursue, to desire, to search for or to endeavor to get." As a believer, our primary goal is to seek the wisdom of God and pursue the leading of the Spirit.

Seeking God's Wisdom

Have you sought God's wisdom for all of your situations in life? God is all-wise; seek Him first for wisdom:

> ...*incline your ear to wisdom, and apply your heart to understanding; yes, if you cry out for discernment, and lift up your voice for understanding, if you seek her as silver, and search for her as for hidden treasures; then you will understand the fear of the* LORD, *and find the knowledge of God. For the* LORD *gives wisdom; from His mouth come knowledge and understanding; He stores up sound wisdom for the upright; He is a shield to those who walk uprightly; He guards the paths of justice, and preserves the way of His saints* [believers in Christ who are set apart for God].
>
> PROVERBS 2:2-8

Christ is the wisdom of God—seek Him!

Seeking God's Peace

In times of anxiety, have you sought God's peace? God would not have you suffer needlessly in turmoil and worry. Jesus promised to give us His peace: *"Peace I leave with you, My peace I give to you; not as the world gives do I give to you. Let not your heart be troubled, neither let it be afraid"* (John 14:27).

When peace is absent from your life, you had better check your heart, life and priorities. If you truly love life and desire to have God's peace, then take the Apostle Peter's sound advice:

> *"He who would love life and see good days, let him refrain his tongue from evil, and his lips from speaking deceit. Let him turn away from evil and do good; let him seek peace and pursue it. For the eyes of the* LORD *are on the righteous, and His ears are*

open to their prayers; but the face of the LORD is against those who do evil."

1 PETER 3:10-12

Seeking God for Faith

Have you sought God to help strengthen your faith? Paul the Apostle exhorts us:

But without faith it is impossible to please Him, for he who comes to God must believe that He is, and that He is a rewarder of those who diligently seek Him.

HEBREWS 11:6

In building up your faith, know that *faith comes by hearing, and hearing by the word of God* (Romans 10:17). Think on the Scriptures that speak of those pilgrims of old who lived by faith. They sought a heavenly reward—a heavenly homeland—a city:

These [the saints of old] *all died in faith, not having received the promises, but having seen them afar off were assured of them, embraced them and confessed that they were strangers and pilgrims on the earth. For those who say such things declare plainly that they seek a homeland. And truly if they had called to mind that country from which they had come out, they would have had opportunity to return. But now they desire a better, that is, a heavenly country. Therefore God is not ashamed to be called their God, for He has prepared a city for them.*

HEBREWS 11:13-16

We are strangers and pilgrims on this earth, living by faith, knowing that we are just passing through on our way to our eternal home.

Seeking God's Righteousness

We must seek first the kingdom of God and His righteousness—not our righteousness. Our righteousness is as filthy rags (Isaiah 64:6). Righteousness can only be gained by placing our faith and trust in Jesus. He is the One who came and died on the Cross to pay the penalty for our sins and make us righteous before Him.

Jesus has prepared a place for us where we are going to live with Him forever and ever. The righteous will inherit a kingdom where Jesus will rule and reign. He is the One who will create a new heaven and a new earth. With that in mind, it would be wise for Christians to seek God first and His righteousness in all circumstances. Our lives need to be perfectly aligned with His will.

While on this earth, you may lose your job, but you need to keep an eternal perspective. God wants believers to be fully dependent on Him. Instead of allowing God to work in the situation, will you begin to murmur and complain, thinking about the people who did not like you, even to the point of getting in the way of God? What if God in His righteousness allowed this to happen so He can move you into a better job? Be open to the Holy Spirit. Remember, God opens and closes doors. He is the One who gives, and He is the One who takes away.

When I read about prophecy in Matthew 24, I realize we are living in the last days. Many things will happen: pestilence, a shortage of food, famine and earthquakes—all these things. It is the beginning of sorrows—the beginning of the end. How in the world are people going to survive a failing economy when they do not make enough on their jobs? Believers can become very anxious, maybe even fearful and afraid, but God is righteous and is working out all things for the good of those who believe on Him.

Paul reminds us in Romans 8:28: *And we know that all things work together for good to those who love God, to those who are the called according to His purpose.* Not our purpose, His purpose. The Apostle Peter also reminds us: *Therefore humble yourselves under the mighty hand of God, that He may exalt you in due time, casting all your care upon Him, for He cares for you* (1 Peter 5:6-7). Listen, God loves and cares for us, so we need to continue forward in seeking God and His righteousness, no matter what happens.

The Rewards of the Righteous

Place God first in everything, including your giving! By faith, give to God what belongs to God, and He promises to take care of you:

> *"Bring all the tithes into the storehouse, that there may be food in My house, and try Me now in this," says the LORD of hosts, "if I will not open for you the windows of heaven and pour out for you such blessing that there will not be room enough to receive it."*

> MALACHI 3:10

When you place God first, and then you go out to work, or wherever you go during your day, you will have His wisdom, His peace and His righteousness. God will be at the helm of your life—leading, providing and guiding your steps of faith. In fact, you will reap abundant, spiritual blessings.

Many times, the reason people are not receiving blessings from the Lord is because they are not giving for the building of God's kingdom. At times, God will take away from our finances because we have not placed Him first. How can we expect to reap His benefits when we are not giving to the work of the Lord?

> *"Will a man rob God? Yet you have robbed Me! But you say, 'In what way have we robbed You?' In tithes and offerings. You are cursed with a curse, for you have robbed Me, even this whole nation."*

> MALACHI 3:8-9

Christians are to seek first His kingdom and His righteousness in all that they do and let God take care of our needs.

Be Christ-Centered

If God is not first in your life, then what has taken first place? Are you going about life thinking about yourself and not others? Christians can become self-centered, but as believers, they need to be Christ-centered instead. Self-centeredness is not to be a characteristic of a true Christian.

The main point Jesus pressed in His sermon was: *"...seek first the kingdom of God and His righteousness, and all these things shall be added to you"* (Matthew 6:33). The Word of God is so clear. Seek first God's kingdom, not your own kingdom! His kingdom! It is important to get this priority right—God's purposes are always first. Then what things shall be added to you—money? No, not always, because God often blesses us in spiritual ways.

Look into your heart and determine what will truly be first in your life. I often challenge people to get seven pieces of paper and, for seven days, write down what they are doing from the time they get up in the morning to when they go to bed in the evening. At the end of the week, examine those seven pieces of paper, and you will see if they are seeking first the kingdom of God or not.

If you examine the life of David, you will see a man who constantly placed God first. David was a man after God's own heart. His highest priority, even during difficult times, was to seek the Lord. He desired more than anything else to have an intimate relationship with God:

> *O God, You are my God; early will I seek You; my soul thirsts for You; my flesh longs for You in a dry and thirsty land where there is no water. So I have looked for You in the sanctuary, to see Your power and Your glory.*

> PSALM 63:1-2

As David sought the Lord, God gave him great depth of understanding. He was able to come to a place of peaceful perspective in life:

> *Do not fret because of evildoers, nor be envious of the workers of iniquity. For they shall soon be cut down like the grass, and wither as the green herb. Trust in the LORD, and do good; dwell in the land, and feed on His faithfulness. Delight yourself also in the LORD, and He shall give you the desires of your heart. Commit your way to the LORD, trust also in Him, and He shall bring it to pass.*
>
> PSALM 37:1-5

In your life, like David, seek the Lord first. Then you will gain the right perspective in life. Why not delight yourself in God and feed on His faithfulness? As you place your trust in the Lord and set your mind to do good, He will give you great wisdom and understanding. He alone can give you the desires of your heart and fulfill His intended promises for your life.

GOD HOLDS OUR TOMORROWS — Matthew 6:34

"Therefore do not worry about tomorrow, for tomorrow will worry about its own things. Sufficient for the day is its own trouble."

We never know what tomorrow holds—but God holds all our tomorrows. Major calamities may come into our lives—tragedies and sorrows—but remember God is always in control. If God is for you, then who can be against you? You do not have to worry about your life—about tomorrow; it will take care of itself. Just take life one day at a time.

An important principle Christians must take hold of was taught by Jesus to His disciples. They were to abide in Him: "*Abide in Me, and I in you*" (John 15:4). Believers must abide in Christ day by day, not month by month or year by year. Honestly, we can only handle one day at a time, not tomorrow or even years ahead of us into the future. We would probably die of worry if we did that!

Christ's *Sermon of Sermons* inspires us to be wise, to seek first the kingdom of God, and to do His will—then everything else will fall into place. In these incredible last days, seek the Lord, pray, and exercise your Christian faith!

12

A MEASURED JUDGMENT

MATTHEW 7:1-5

In the previous chapters, Jesus spoke about the attitudes a disciple of Christ should exhibit. He then taught practical lessons about life's priorities. He had also given His followers the needed reassurance and comfort for all of life's worries. If His disciples trusted in the divine capabilities of their heavenly Father, they need not worry about earthly provisions. He was able to take care of their every need.

As Jesus continued to teach His sermon, He wanted His disciples to retain within their minds the eternal perspective He had formerly taught them—*seek first the kingdom of God.* Jesus, from the very beginning, taught His disciples in a very gentle manner. Now as Jesus concluded His teachings, He became very serious.

JUDGE NOT — Matthew 7:1-2

> "Judge not, that you be not judged. For with what judgment you judge, you will be judged; and with the measure you use, it will be measured back to you."

Jesus spoke with unchallenged authority. There was a common problem that He needed to address. He knew people were very quick to judge others unrighteously, not according to godly principles found in the Word of God. Jesus gave such a serious warning for every child of God to heed. Those called to be His disciples were never to wrongly judge anyone. Why? The same judgment, righteous or unrighteous, they pronounced on others would have a way of coming back on them.

The word *judge* means "to be critical in your judgment—criticize." Jesus exhorted His followers to stop judging, stop criticizing, and stop condemning people. Those who judged and criticized others were spiritually blind, inconsistent, self-righteous people who lacked love.

Dietrich Bonhoeffer gave us this honest insight: Judging others makes us blind, whereas love is illuminating. By judging others we blind ourselves to our own evil and to the grace which others are just as entitled to as we are.[9] We are all guilty of judging others.

The phrase Jesus used *"that you be not judged"* means God will judge a person on the imperfections of their harsh judgment against other people. God's judgment will reflect the same standard of measurement given toward a person whom they have continually harassed in faulty judgment. They will be judged by the law of equal sin and will receive the greater condemnation. They will stand before the Lord on the Day of Judgment to be judged in the same manner they have judged other people.

Paul the Apostle also gave strong words of warning on the same issue of judging others:

> *Therefore you are inexcusable, O man, whoever you are who judge, for in whatever you judge another you condemn yourself; for you who judge practice the same things.*

ROMANS 2:1

God will judge those who practice judgment on other people.

The Apostle James declared:

> *Do not speak evil of one another, brethren. He who speaks evil of a brother and judges his brother, speaks evil of the law and*

judges the law. But if you judge the law, you are not a doer of the law but a judge. There is one Lawgiver, who is able to save and to destroy. Who are you to judge another?

JAMES 4:11-12

As a child of God, check your heart. You must adhere to the Word of God concerning judging others—before God, you will be held accountable.

SPECK FINDING — Matthew 7:3-4

"And why do you look at the speck in your brother's eye, but do not consider the plank in your own eye? Or how can you say to your brother, 'Let me remove the speck from your eye'; and look, a plank is in your own eye?"

Jesus' words always brought people to the truth. He caused them to see the pretense of judging by using a perfect illustration. They were to look at the tiny speck in someone else's eye compared to the obvious plank—beam—in their own eye! Jesus basically said to them, "Before you point out a fault in someone else's life, you had better take a really good look at your own life first." With this simple truth, Jesus helped His disciples understand how incredibly wrong it was to judge and criticize others.

Pastor Chuck Smith's assisting pastor, Romaine, from Calvary Chapel Costa Mesa, California, always used this illustration to combat judging among believers. He said: "When you point your finger at someone else, then you have three fingers pointing back at you!" That is so true! If you find fault with others, you had better first look at yourself in the mirror before pointing your finger at anybody else. Who are you to judge, condemn and point your finger at other people? Did you forget that by God's grace, you are a saved sinner like everybody else? The Apostle James cuts through deception and brings to light the forgetfulness of knowing yourself:

> But be doers of the word, and not hearers only, deceiving yourselves. For if anyone is a hearer of the word and not a doer, he is like a man observing his natural face in a mirror; for he observes himself, goes away, and immediately forgets what kind of man he was. But he who looks into the perfect law of liberty and continues in it, and is not a forgetful hearer but a doer of the work, this one will be blessed in what he does.
>
> JAMES 1:22-25

People are quick to judge, but can they really know what is going on in the heart of someone? They are able to outwardly see people's emotions and reactions, but they do not know their hearts. Again, with the same standard that you use to judge others, it will return to bite you—big time. It is so dangerous to be judging other people. You do not want God to harshly judge you!

Do You Have a Critical Spirit?

It is so easy to judge and criticize! Criticizing can become such a bad habit. This sinful practice is a major problem with Christians inside the church and with nonbelievers outside of the church. Think about it! Have you ever noticed those who love to point out every little, negative detail in another person's life? That is having a critical spirit.

A person who has a critical spirit will bring division into the church. They are determined to destroy the characters of other people. They can criticize a pastor, an elder, a leader and anyone in the congregation.

Those who judge unrighteously will tear people apart spiritually. They break down their character and lives. Are you a critical person that judges other people? Do you pick people apart until you have totally torn down their character? After you tear people down, who will build these people back up?

As a Christian, how do you expect people to hear what you have to say if you are ceaselessly critical toward them? Judging and criticizing will condemn a person. Others will not accept what you say. No way! People will become mad and bitter toward you. They will not want to speak to you, see you, or be near you—you will have pushed them away.

This problem of judging is also outside the church. Nonbelievers living in this world have given themselves what they think is a perfect excuse for not attending church—they have judged that in the church, there are far too many hypocrites, so they criticize us. That is a lame excuse. It could be that these very same people are more than likely the biggest hypocrites of all! The truth is they do not want to go to church and hear from God and be convicted of sin.

The Character of the Criticizer

Critical people can be found everywhere. Jesus' question, *"And why do you look at the speck in your brother's eye, but do not consider the plank in your own eye?"* reveals that the criticizer is *self-deceived*. When confronted about their judgmental spirit, in response they dismiss it as a gift of exhortation from God or give another vain excuse. They fail to see what other people see in them, and, much less, what God sees. They are blind to the truth of their own sinful nature. They choose to ignore God's Word.

Honestly, if you are offended about a believer confronting you about your life, that is pride. If you cannot receive from them, then how in the world are you going to receive from the Lord? Examine yourself first through God's Word! The problem many times is you are not in intimate fellowship with God through His Word. These Scriptures will correct a criticizer's self-deception:

> *The way of a fool is right in his own eyes, but he who heeds counsel is wise.*

> PROVERBS 12:15

Most men will proclaim each his own goodness, but who can find a faithful man?

PROVERBS 20:6

Every way of a man is right in his own eyes, but the LORD weighs the hearts.

PROVERBS 21:2

Anytime someone comes to you in love with something they have seen in your life, be open to the truth. Repent of your ways and allow God to bring about needed change. If someone is critical toward me, I like to learn from what they have to say. I need to be open to what the Holy Spirit has to impress upon my heart as people minister to me. I listen to the truth, but I disregard anything that is not of the Lord. That way, God can continue to use my life.

Self-Righteousness

The person who habitually stands in judgment of others while ignoring their own sin is guilty of *self-righteousness*. It is possible for a person to come to a place where they falsely believe they are practically perfect. Everyone else's opinions are wrong—except for theirs.

A criticizer will even separate themselves from other people. As they judge them and pick at their faults, they find excuses to no longer fellowship with them. They set themselves up as if they are God. They may even take pleasure from others who see them in a higher position of command. No one has the right to place themselves above others. God is not a respecter of persons. His unconditional love is for everyone.

When someone criticizes another person, they are, in fact, making the obvious statement, "I am better than you are!" They feel they are above everyone else. In comparison with the faulty lives of others, they view themselves as a holy person, and everyone else is markedly below them. Really! We are all sinners! Jesus Christ is the only perfect One! Every day we all "miss the mark." Can you not grasp the truth of Romans 3:10-12?

> "There is none righteous, no, not one; there is none who understands; there is none who seeks after God. They have all turned aside; they have together become unprofitable; there is none who does good, no, not one."

Resist the urge to judge others. It will hurt you and your relationships with other people. If you continue to have a judgmental attitude, you are going to hinder the work of God in your own life.

The Standard of the Cross

Christians can succumb to criticism when individuals do not agree with their views. They begin to compare themselves with others. Scripture declares: ...*But they* [those who commend themselves], *measuring themselves by themselves, and comparing themselves among themselves, are not wise* (2 Corinthians 10:12).

Christians should not compare themselves to each other, but should receive everyone in Christ, no matter how different these individuals are. A.W. Tozer made the Cross of Christ the standard of judgment when he said:

> "The cross stands high above the opinions of men—and to that cross all opinions must come at last for judgment."[10]

When you set up your standards around the Cross, you will be able to love people unconditionally—bottom line.

Do you remember the hippie days? Many churches were not receiving the hippies into their congregations. People did not like the way they dressed: the sandals, flared, ripped jeans, bare, dirty feet, big beards and mustaches. They looked so different!

When hippies walked into some churches, the first thing people did to them was to try to change their appearance. They wanted to make them look exactly like them. These individuals would not accept the hippies; they could not understand how they could bring dishonor into a place of worship with bare feet and in ragged clothing.

They were far too concerned with their outward appearance and never sought to understand these sincere lost souls who wanted a refuge in the house of God. Some people were outspoken in their condemnation of them. Yet they forgot about the inward—a person's changed heart. It is not how a person looks on the outside that counts; it is what has happened on the inside. How many times do we misjudge people? God help us never to forget that.

Even though people are tattooed, have long hair, or they have come from off the street, you cannot judge the outer appearance of anyone. You do not know what God has done within the heart of a person. Often it is not until you talk to them, and actually come to know them, that you witness their spirituality. They may really know God, and may desire a deeper knowledge of Him—so beautiful.

How can sinners come into the kingdom of God when people in the Church are critically judging them? Instead of drawing them to Christ, their critical attitude pushes them away from Him. Christians are called to invite sinners to know Jesus. That can only happen when they see how a genuine believer acts, speaks and lives.

Our standard must always be the Cross—Christ's humility, His servanthood, and His death on the Cross for the forgiveness of sins. He gives us an example to follow:

> *Let nothing be done through selfish ambition or conceit, but in lowliness of mind let each esteem others better than himself. Let each of you look out not only for his own interests, but also for the interests of others.*

> *Let this mind be in you which was also in Christ Jesus, who, being in the form of God, did not consider it robbery to be equal with God, but made Himself of no reputation, taking the form of a bondservant, and coming in the likeness of men. And being found in appearance as a man, He humbled Himself and became obedient to the point of death, even the death of the cross.*
>
> PHILIPPIANS 2:3-8

If you are a critical person, instead of placing yourself above people, humble yourself and begin to serve others instead. If we are going to be like Christ, we need to be loving and kind. Jesus is the *One* who did not criticize or point His finger. He is the *One* who came to show us the way through His love. He is the *One* who forgave us—pointing us to the Cross. In the Cross we see the example of death to self. When you learn to follow the example of Christ, you will no longer be judging and criticizing other people.

Destructive Criticism within the Family

As Christians, at times our old sinful nature can rise up. When we yield to our flesh, we can become extremely critical of those around us—a husband, wife or children.

Think of how many children are intimidated by a parent's critical actions or words. A father or mother who repeatedly puts down their children will make them feel they can never do anything right. Instead of building them up, they tear them down. Critical parents destroy their children! If they do not stop criticizing, they will experience major problems within their families.

Some husbands, often because of pride, will not receive the truth spoken to them in love from their wives. They respond to them harshly, saying, "I am the boss; I really do not care what you have to say to me," when, in reality, they should be open to accept what is said from their spouse. Believe me, our families know us best. They eat with us and sleep in the same house! It is humbling when a child comes to their father to say, "Daddy, why are you so mean? Why are you always putting down Mom?" That is humbling, but God will even use a child to get a father's attention.

When a husband and wife constantly criticize each other, their marriage will not thrive; it may eventually head toward separation and divorce. Husbands and wives should have an attitude of approachableness. There should be no pride. Instead, there should be thankfulness toward anyone who comes to them with a loving exhortation—family member or non-family.

Maybe as a child, you have been cruelly criticized and put down by your mother or father. As an adult, you have allowed a deep-rooted bitterness to grow in your heart. When you eventually marry and have children of your own, you may begin to follow the same pattern of behavior—you will criticize your wife and children.

A wife can criticize her husband in the same way. This will only create a great deal of friction within the marriage. This is not what Jesus has taught us to do. Husbands are commanded by the Lord to love their wives, and wives are commanded to reverence their husbands (Ephesians 5:25, 33). As a believer, you are a new creation in Christ— old things have passed away, and all things have been made brand new (2 Corinthians 5:17).

Parents should take a close examination of their lives. Clearly, they cannot be one with God and one with each other if they are always insulting each other. It is hypocritical. A husband or wife will have to ask themselves, "Am I really a Christian?"

I would pray that you humble yourself and tell those you have severely hurt that you are sorry. Make things right with your spouse and children. Be loving and kind. Always try to catch yourself before you open your mouth. Think before you speak! Then God will bless you!

Time for Self-Examination

The criticizer lacks self-examination. He or she has failed to look deep within their own personal life. They are very inconsistent. They are so busy inspecting other people, they forget it is God who is the One who judges and examines everyone's hearts. They must ask themselves, "Are my actions righteous or not righteous?"

The Apostle Paul calls every believer to a place of self-examination:

> *Examine yourselves as to whether you are in the faith. Test yourselves. Do you not know yourselves, that Jesus Christ is in you?—unless indeed you are disqualified.*

2 CORINTHIANS 13:5

The word *disqualified* means "to be put on the shelf." A person went to the library to check out multiple books, when all of a sudden they found a book all on its own on the corner, top shelf. As they reached to pick it up, it was full of dust—it had not been read in some time. That is just like the criticizer! They, like the book, can no longer be used—nobody will want to use them, not even God. Have your actions caused you to be disqualified? Could it be that your life can be compared to an unused book collecting dust in the library?

If you are not willing to be fully surrendered to the Lord, you will continue to criticize until disqualified, and you will remain unusable. It is not until you take a good look at your heart, repent, and admit to the Lord that you are guilty of being critical of others, that God can begin to do a new work in your life.

REMOVE THE PLANK — Matthew 7:5

> "Hypocrite! First remove the plank from your own eye, and then you will see clearly to remove the speck from your brother's eye."

These are the words of *gentle* Jesus. He powerfully called out the sin of hypocrisy in the lives of those who judged others. They had played the part of a hypocrite! Jesus taught that before a person judged someone else, they had better first look at their own lives! If they did, they would find a huge plank in their own eye, while trying to point out a speck in another person's eye.

The first priority is to remove the plank from your own eye. Then you will see clearly who the problem is. If you are the one not getting along with people because you are criticizing them, then you are the problem!

Christians cannot be hypocrites. When they make a stand in judgment against someone else, they act as if they have no sin themselves, when in reality, their sin is just as bad or even worse than the person's sin they are judging.

People first need to recognize the huge beam—the fault in their own eye—in their own lives, that needs to be taken out, before they can even attempt to remove the tiny speck—the fault from within their brother's eye—in their life! What is the real attitude Jesus would have Christians display before making a judgment? Love! Our judgment should be a righteous judgment governed by God.

The Sin of Hypocrisy

Throughout the Gospels, Jesus preached, taught and ministered to people. The pious, religious elite—the Pharisees and Sadducees that formed the Sanhedrin— (the ancient Jewish court system), hated and criticized Jesus. They were hypocritical, and at every opportunity, they would criticize and falsely judge Him.

The Pharisees and Sadducees strictly kept to their religious traditions and accused Jesus of breaking their ceremonial Laws. They were hypocrites who brought people into bondage by adding their own hypocritical laws, whereas the Gospel set people free.

In authority, Jesus revealed to them that sinful defilement came from within the heart:

> *"...those things which proceed out of the mouth come from the heart, and they defile a man. For out of the heart proceed evil thoughts, murders, adulteries, fornications, thefts, false witness, blasphemies. These are the things which defile a man, but to eat with unwashed hands does not defile a man."*
>
> MATTHEW 15:18-20

Hypocritical people not only judge and criticize others, but they often harbor bitterness and express anger and wrath as they habitually speak evil of other people. It could very well be they are trying to justify the things they are doing in their own lives. Judging and criticizing can become an outlet to hurt others. What is revealed to others is the hatefulness of their hearts. All these sins grieve the Holy Spirit of God:

> *And do not grieve the Holy Spirit of God, by whom you were sealed for the day of redemption. Let all bitterness, wrath, anger, clamor, and evil speaking be put away from you, with all malice. And be kind to one another, tenderhearted, forgiving one another, even as God in Christ forgave you.*
>
> EPHESIANS 4:30-32

Did you know that you can bring pain to the Person of the Holy Spirit? How do you view yourself? Until you see your faults and, in meekness, humble yourself in true repentance, God cannot operate through your life. As Christians, we must love and forgive people—that is the Christian life! Never go back to criticizing and judging people again, so God can use you.

Righteous Judgments

Christians need to be able to discern and make godly, right judgments within the church. In Matthew 18:15-17, Jesus gave the standards for judging righteously. When a believer has committed an obvious and visible sin, then a brother or sister in Christ could make a godly judgment.

After a time of prayer, a fellow believer can take the initiative and, in love, approach the offender. As they speak privately together, the situation is kept between them and God. The issue remains between them alone. It is nobody else's business.

It is important to explain the sinful behavior you have seen in their life. Allow the Holy Spirit to check their hearts and convict them. He is the only One who can change people's hearts. If they refuse to repent, then biblically, you are to tell the leadership of the church. Then the elders will also speak privately to that person found to be in sin.

I know there are churches that will tell the entire congregation about the sin of a person. I do not believe that Matthew 18:15-17 is meant to infect the whole church with the details of anyone's sin. The only time I would say anything to the congregation is to warn them about someone whose rebellion is affecting the church or is teaching heresy. Then the body of Christ has to know, and I will tell them from the pulpit.

When a person has been spoken to by the leadership of the church, and they remain self-willed and unrepentant, having no change of heart, then they will be asked to leave the church. They can no longer fellowship with other believers in the body of Christ.

However, if a person truly repents, restoration can take place. God's purpose is always to restore those who have fallen into sin. The Apostle Paul encourages mature Christians to have the right heart attitude in the process of someone's restoration. Beforehand, in wisdom, Paul advised self-examination and humility:

> *Brethren, if a man is overtaken in any trespass, you who are spiritual restore such a one in a spirit of gentleness, considering*

yourself lest you also be tempted. Bear one another's burdens, and so fulfill the law of Christ. For if anyone thinks himself to be something, when he is nothing, he deceives himself.

GALATIANS 6:1-3

That is the biblical nature of church discipline; it is never to destroy, but to restore. Those who repent and desire accountability are restored back into fellowship.

Merciful Judgment

Keep watch over yourself. Do not make a preconceived judgment over the lives of other people. Have an open heart toward all those who come to share their problems with you. Love them, pray for them, and show them mercy. It is Jesus' desire that His followers show God's mercy to others:

"Therefore be merciful, just as your Father also is merciful. Judge not, and you shall not be judged. Condemn not, and you shall not be condemned. Forgive, and you will be forgiven. Give, and it will be given to you: good measure, pressed down, shaken together, and running over will be put into your bosom. For with the same measure that you use, it will be measured back to you."

LUKE 6:36-38

Jesus gave this parallel passage in the Sermon on the Mount: *"Judge not, that you be not judged. For with what judgment you judge, you will be judged; and with the measure you use, it will be measured back to you"* (Matthew 7:1-2).

Understand clearly that *...judgment is without mercy to the one who has shown no mercy. Mercy triumphs over judgment* (James 2:13). If you desire for God to show you mercy, then show mercy to others.

13

THE GOSPEL, PRAYER, AND THE PATH TO LIFE

MATTHEW 7:6-14

Jesus gave a serious teaching in His sermon that applies directly to us today. He previously warned His disciples not to judge others. Now He spoke on several different topics: the preciousness of the Gospel, praying for good things that God desires to give to us, treating others with honor, and instruction to the gateway of heaven.

PRESENTING THE GOSPEL — Matthew 7:6

"Do not give what is holy to the dogs; nor cast your pearls before swine, lest they trample them under their feet, and turn and tear you in pieces."

Jesus warned His disciples not to give that which was holy to the dogs nor cast their pearls before swine. What did Jesus mean when He taught this? He taught His disciples to use discernment when sharing the Gospel with people. In His teaching, He gave a vivid picture of a person who sincerely tried to give God's *holy* Word to those who violently rejected it—to *dogs*. They treated the holy Word of God in an unholy manner. It would be as futile as giving what is holy to dogs.

The *dogs* Jesus referred to were wild scavengers that roamed in packs in the city. These ravenous dogs would go into the trash pits to look for any food. Can you imagine coming across a pack of wild, starving dogs? If you offered them a tasty piece of meat, they would turn to attack and tear you into pieces!

The disciples needed to be cautious not to cast their pearls—the beautiful Gospel of Jesus Christ—to those who would stomp on it. For the average person, pearls are very expensive to buy. The Greek word *margaritári* means "pearl." Pearls are obtained from many places. The Persian Gulf is known as the Pearl of Paradise, and in the Indian Ocean, South Sea pearls are taken from gold-lipped or silver-lipped oysters. If the disciples shared with people who did not want to hear the Gospel, it would be like casting priceless pearls before swine to be trampled under their muddy feet!

If you discern that someone is not interested in hearing the Gospel of truth, and they will abhor it, you do not have to cast your pearls before swine. The truth is, there are people who you just cannot share the wonderful things of God with.

In the Old Testament, swine are identified as unclean animals to the Jews. Remember, Jews could not eat pork. Think how sin utterly defiles a person. They are unclean! If we look at the world today, it is full of unclean sinners who often revile the Gospel of Jesus Christ.

Think about your close circle of friends and family. When you have tried to tell them about God, did any of them become offended, aggravated or even aggressive? Many Christians have been violently assaulted because of the Gospel. In the early Church, under the rule of the Roman Empire, millions of Christians were killed.

However, it is believed that even more Christians have died for the Gospel of Jesus Christ in the 21st century. Unfortunately, we just do not hear about it. Yet it is clearly recorded for those who are willing to search out the truth. Christians are being trampled on, maligned, persecuted and martyred at the hands of those who have despised them and the Word of God. They hate the messenger and the message of the Gospel.

According to the 2022 World Watch List (WWL), the latest annual account from Open Doors, a nondenominational mission that supports persecuted Christians, named the top ten countries where Christians are the most persecuted for their faith: Afghanistan, North Korea, Somalia, Libya, Yemen, Eritrea, Nigeria, Pakistan, Iran and India.

David Curry, president and CEO of Open Doors USA, stated about the rise of persecution in China: "The Chinese government is committing unparalleled human rights crimes against Christian citizens and seeking to wipe religious sentiment from its country."[11] It is well-known that Christians in China have sought refuge in underground churches, as they are watched, harassed and unfairly arrested.

Gordon Conwell's Center for the Study of Global Christianity reported on the persecution of Christians, which found that as many as 90,000 Christians died for their faith in 2016. The study gave further statistics that one Christian every six minutes was killed in that same year. The cost of a Christian presenting the Gospel to others can be the price of his life! It cost Christ the shedding of His precious blood to bring mankind the forgiveness of man's sin.

Again, in Matthew 7:6, *casting your pearls before swine* refers to giving the Gospel of Christ to those who will trample on it. Many will reject the beautiful pearl of the Gospel. If only they would heed the prophet Isaiah's life-giving-words: *"Come now, and let us reason together,"* says the Lord, *"Though your sins are like scarlet, they shall be as white as snow; though they are red like crimson, they shall be as wool"* (Isaiah 1:18). This is the pearl of the Gospel that they are trampling on.

Interestingly, the Church who delivers the pearl of the Gospel to sinners is referred to in the Word of God as the *pearl of great price* in Matthew 13:45-46. For many believers, the rejection of the Gospel is taken as a personal affront. Yet those who choose to reject it are, in fact, not rejecting the believer; they are rejecting Christ and eternal life which is freely given to man by the shedding of the blood of Jesus Christ for the forgiveness of man's sins.

The Apostle Paul declared: *For I am not ashamed of the gospel of Christ, for it is the power of God to salvation for everyone who believes, for the Jew first and also for the Greek* (Romans 1:16). The Gospel message is God's gift of salvation to anyone who will receive it.

Knowing hardened hearts, Jesus would refuse to give the religious elite the pearls of the Gospel. Instead, He would strongly rebuke them. Spiritual truths were revealed to those who had an open heart to understand them. Jesus often used parables—stories that speak to people about things kept secret from the foundations of the world—to explain the mysteries of the kingdom of heaven (Matthew 13:13-15).

Many of the hypocritical, religious elite—the Pharisees, Sadducees and scribes—were fools who remained blind to these truths (Matthew 23:19). Foolishly, they openly rejected Christ. Secretly they spied on Him in hopes of accusing Him of any unlawful act. They were so far from understanding anything Jesus taught, even to the point of naming the Son of God, Satan! Jesus warned them that they were getting close to the blasphemy of the Holy Spirit.

Numerous people remain in sin and scoff at Christ. They wickedly revile Him by continually rejecting His Word. They reject Christ and blaspheme God. When a person continually rejects the Gospel of Jesus Christ, they can cross a fine line, and because of their rejection of the Holy Spirit's conviction in their lives, not even God can save them— they are done:

> *"Therefore I say to you, every sin and blasphemy will be forgiven men, but the blasphemy against the Spirit will not be forgiven men. Anyone who speaks a word against the Son of Man, it will be forgiven him; but whoever speaks against the Holy Spirit, it will not be forgiven him, either in this age or in the age to come."*
>
> MATTHEW 12:31-32

The Gospel message is so precious, and it should not be taken lightly. Yet many people who do not have God's peace in their lives still remain so obstinate, wanting nothing to do with Jesus Christ. Instead, they forfeit the grace and peace of God for an eternity separated from Him!

Backsliders

There are those who have received the Gospel and were saved, washed and cleansed from the filth of their sin, yet they returned to their sinful living. They have become backslidden.

Like Jesus, it is the Apostle Peter who chose to use a similar striking description of dogs and pigs to make a strong point. He mentioned the foul habits of pigs wallowing in mud and dogs licking up what they have just vomited: *...it has happened to them according to the true proverb: "A dog returns to his own vomit," and "a sow, having washed, to her wallowing in the mire"* (2 Peter 2:22).

Think for a moment about a pig. If you take a pig and wash him in the bathtub, what happens the minute he is released? The pig goes right back into the mud! Those who own dogs know that dogs left to themselves will eat their own vomit! This is a true description of those who backslide and return to the things they were once delivered from—sad.

When you know the preciousness of the Gospel, how can you reject its message? You have tasted the truth! You have been given God's holy Word. It is something so holy, pure and of great worth—like a pearl. When obeyed, God's Word sanctifies you; it keeps you clean from sin.

The psalmist declared:

> *How can a young man cleanse his way? By taking heed according to Your word. With my whole heart I have sought You; oh, let me not wander from Your commandments! Your word I have hidden in my heart, that I might not sin against You.*

> PSALM 119:9-11

Believers need to be careful not to once more become enslaved to sin. Fear God and truly obey Him, as *to whom much is given, from him much will be required* on the Day of Judgment (Luke 12:48).

Our Duty to Share the Gospel

When Jesus preached the Gospel among the multitudes, many responded and followed Him. Others followed Jesus for a time, but only because of the miracles and wonders He performed. How many ended up hating Jesus, shouting for Him to be crucified? People in this world still hate Jesus and the Gospel.

Christians have such a passion in their hearts to see their friends and family saved. Christians have a duty to share the Good News, but it is important to be sensitive on how the Gospel is presented to others. Christ's message should be communicated in love. People need to know the grace and love of God so they do not feel condemned. Never force or corner people with the Gospel. Allow the Holy Spirit to bring conviction to their lives and lead them to Christ. The Holy Spirit is the only One who can convict people of sin and their need for Christ.

Remember, it was the work of the Holy Spirit that convicted you and me! However, if a person does not want to hear the good news of the Gospel, then a believer is under no obligation to give it to them. There are people who do not want to hear the Gospel—period.

On one occasion in a restaurant, a waitress who was a single mother came to take our order. There was a slight open door to share with her about the Gospel. When I saw she was a little resistant to hear, I stopped. I knew not to force the Gospel on her. Yet she began to open up to my son Ryan, and she candidly told him about her problems. He fully shared the way of salvation with her.

Prayer for the lost is so important. When a Christian fervently prays for someone, they need to ask the Lord to intercept their life and convict them of sin. It is only through the conviction of the Holy Spirit that they can receive Jesus Christ as their Savior. They have a free will to choose to accept or reject the Gospel. Pray that God will open their eyes, touch their hearts, and rescue them with the Gospel of grace. He can reach them and answer your persistent prayers. Then they, too, will be able to understand the things of God.

One of the greatest witnesses to a nonbeliever is observing a Christian who is a living example of the life of Christ. It is not by preaching. Instead, as they watch that Christian's life and see their genuine faith lived out in front of them, they witness firsthand how a believer in Christ has truly been transformed. However, if a Christian becomes a bad witness, a nonbeliever may question the validity of their conversion. Disappointed, they may say, "I thought you were a Christian transformed by the power of the Holy Spirit?"

Jesus encountered Matthew, a tax collector, and called him to follow Him. Matthew did so without hesitation. When Jesus was invited to dinner at Matthew's house, all eyes were upon Him as He sat among sinners. However, Jesus did not preach the Gospel to them; He sat and ate with them. Those present must have also witnessed Matthew's transformed life. He was transformed by the power of the Gospel of Jesus Christ (Matthew 9:9-13).

I have found that the greatest example to those who do not know Christ is to just live the Christian life. They will see your transformation, and ask, "What do you have that I do not have?" They see the joy and fullness that you have in your heart compared to the deep emptiness in their hearts.

I believe with all my heart that is why people in this world drink, commit adultery and fornicate; they are never truly satisfied, even though they may have material wealth. That void will only grow and become deeper and deeper. It is not until they come to Jesus that they will be satisfied—fully and completely.

ASK, SEEK, KNOCK — Matthew 7:7-8

> "Ask, and it will be given to you; seek, and you will find; knock, and it will be opened to you. For everyone who asks receives, and he who seeks finds, and to him who knocks it will be opened."

Jesus gave three important actions His disciples needed to do while in prayer: ask, seek and knock. Our Lord spoke of having a life of prayer that continually seeks after God. Interestingly, in the Greek language, these terms give to us an even deeper meaning. *Ask, seek and knock* simply means "keep asking, keep seeking, keep knocking"—do not quit.

A child of God must comprehend that the answer to their prayers might not come when they want it to happen. Our prayers to our heavenly Father should not be demanding or conditional—in accordance to what we want. The purpose of prayer is to always align ourselves in agreement to His will and not our own.

Be aware of a dangerous false teaching found in certain churches. False teachers have influenced some people to believe in "positive confession." They teach that whatever you ask God for in prayer, it will come into existence. Not so!

As a child of God, be patient and wait on the Lord for His answers to your prayers. As you pray, God opens and closes doors for you. Again, prayer should be on the basis of God's will. Be open to the answer God wants to give you according to His timing.

Consider that sometimes our prayers are answered while we remain on earth, and at other times, when we are in heaven. Did you know your prayers continually ascend to the throne room of God in heaven? A glorious picture is given of this truth in Revelation 5:8, where golden bowls full of incense are referenced as the prayers of the saints in heaven.

OUR FATHER GIVES GOOD THINGS — Matthew 7:9-11

"Or what man is there among you who, if his son asks for bread, will give him a stone? Or if he asks for a fish, will he give him a serpent? If you then, being evil, know how to give good gifts to your children, how much more will your Father who is in heaven give good things to those who ask Him!"

For all those who belong to the kingdom of God, what a wonderful promise is given to them!

This was another illustration that Jesus gave to help His disciples understand that their heavenly Father would hear and answer their prayers. God would give them good things! If a son asked his earthly father for bread, would he give him a stone, saying, "Here, Son, chew on this!" No way! His father would lovingly answer his son's request and give him the bread he needed and asked for!

The good things given to us by our heavenly Father are not in reference to a new car, a new house, or additional money, but in its context, Jesus was referring to the Holy Spirit. Christians need the power of the Holy Spirit to become witnesses for Christ in this world:

"...You shall receive power when the Holy Spirit has come upon you; and you shall be witnesses to Me in Jerusalem, and in all Judea and Samaria, and to the end of the earth."

ACTS 1:8

The power of the Holy Spirit is given to any believer who asks. For a life of power in service for the kingdom of God, ask the Lord to fill you daily with His Holy Spirit. It is important to continue to ask; never stop asking God to fill you with His Holy Spirit. God desires for every believer to be filled with His power.

The fire of the Holy Spirit will never come down upon you unless you are living in obedience to God's Word. How can you pray for more power when you have no power because of your sin? It is hypocritical because you are praying in contradiction to His Word. The only way God can answer your prayers is if you are obedient to His Word, doing the will of God from the heart, and speaking the truth of God. Then the Holy Spirit will do the rest.

In these last days, what do you need to change in your heart so you can become empowered by God's Holy Spirit?

THE GOLDEN RULE — Matthew 7:12

> "Therefore, whatever you want men to do to you, do also to them, for this is the Law and the Prophets."

I am sure you have heard this well-known phrase quoted, "Treat others how you want to be treated." It is called the *Golden Rule*. Jesus taught it to His disciples in a positive way. His followers should treat people with God's love. Buddha also taught this principle, but he communicated it in a negative way: "Hurt not others in ways that you yourself would find hurtful."

Jesus taught practical application in the Sermon on the Mount so simply that it could be easily grasped by those listening. He desired His disciples to follow these life principles. I am sure His teachings were very convicting, and caused His followers to examine their lives. Not only should they live their lives in holiness and consecration, but they were taught to show God's love to everyone.

Consider what else Jesus taught in Matthew 22:37-39:

> " *'You shall love the LORD your God with all your heart, with all your soul, and with all your mind.' This is the first and great*

commandment. And the second is like it: 'You shall love your neighbor as yourself.' On these two commandments hang all the Law and the Prophets."

A righteous, loving, pure life fits the entire Sermon on the Mount. People will be able to read your life like a book. A life of Christian love will speak so much louder than any spoken words. So when there is an opportunity to help others, as Jesus' followers, we are to be motivated by God's love as we put this Golden Rule into practice.

God intends to use our lives tremendously. He desires to pour out His love to a lost and dying world around us. How in the world can we reach people for Jesus Christ if we do not love them? Charles Spurgeon knew Christians were not called to be ordinary men and women; he knew they were to be held to a higher standard of life. He said of this Christian standard:

> "While the golden rule is more admired than practiced by ordinary men, the Christian should always do unto others as he would that they should do unto him...."

This means Christians cannot be judgmental or act maliciously toward people. They are children of the light, and as such, they are to be loving, trustworthy and honest. The lives of Christians should match their beliefs; they must practice what they preach throughout the entire week. Do you treat others the way you would like to be treated?

THE PATH TO LIFE — Matthew 7:13-14

> "Enter by the narrow gate; for wide is the gate and broad is the way that leads to destruction, and there are many who go in by it. Because narrow is the gate and difficult is the way which leads to life, and there are few who find it."

Jesus came down to the nitty gritty meaning of the Gospel—"Who can inherit the kingdom of God?" He made the way so narrow so that not many find it. The entrance is through the narrow gate—it leads to life. Even though God's salvation is a free gift, multitudes of people remain hell-bound, traveling through the wide gate which leads to destruction.

The late Billy Graham, a powerful evangelist of the Gospel of Jesus Christ, encourages sinners on the path leading toward heaven:

> "There are two roads of life, the world's path and God's path. Consider the journey and choose the way of the Lord—the narrow path. Jesus is there and He is the way to heaven."[12]

Which path are you on? Do you need to change your eternal direction?

Sadly, the true way of salvation is often rejected, not accepted. No matter what religion you are—Buddhist, Taoist, Mormon, Jehovah's Witness, Catholic or Protestant—a person must come to God through Jesus Christ, or they will perish: *"For God so loved the world that He gave His only begotten Son, that whoever believes in Him should not perish but have everlasting life"* (John 3:16).

Religion is man's way of trying to reach God through a person's own merits. People try to go around and reach God in other ways, but it is not about religion; it is about relationship. Salvation is found only through Jesus Christ. He is the Bridge Builder—the Mediator between God and man: *For there is one God and one Mediator between God and men, the Man Christ Jesus* (1 Timothy 2:5). Jesus is the only way, the only truth, and the only life (John 14:6).

The Gospel is so simple, yet so many will perish eternally. I believe it is because of their unbelief and lack of faith in accepting Jesus Christ as their Savior. Jesus is mankind's Savior. The name *Jesus* translates to English as *Joshua* and means "God is salvation." The Hebrew name for *Jesus* is *Yeshua* or *Y'shua,* which means "to save, deliver or to rescue." His name reflects His purpose to save us. Imagine, one day at the name of Jesus, every knee should bow, and every tongue should confess that Jesus Christ is Lord (Philippians 2:10-11).

Where Do I Go When I Die?

Most people have questions in their minds about eternity. They wonder, *When I die what really happens to me?* According to the Scriptures, the body dies, but the spirit goes on to live forever. The Apostle Paul helps us to take confident hold of this eternal hope when he said: *We are confident, yes, well pleased rather to be absent from the body and to be present with the Lord* (2 Corinthians 5:8).

Heaven is real. We live our lives by faith with an expectation of an eternal home:

> *Therefore we do not lose heart. Even though our outward man is perishing, yet the inward man is being renewed day by day. For our light affliction, which is but for a moment, is working for us a far more exceeding and eternal weight of glory, while we do not look at the things which are seen, but at the things which are not seen. For the things which are seen are temporary, but the things which are not seen are eternal.*

> 2 CORINTHIANS 4:16-18

Your decision whether or not to accept Christ as your Savior will determine where you spend eternity. If the Holy Spirit has spoken to you, stepped on your toes, and convicted you, then you have two choices. You can either accept God's grace, mercy, love and forgiveness, or you can reject Him. Christ calls you to make a public confession with this promise:

> *"Therefore whoever confesses Me before men, him I will also confess before My Father who is in heaven. But whoever denies Me before men, him I will also deny before My Father who is in heaven."*

> MATTHEW 10:32-33

When you come to Christ, you are forgiven of your sins. The Holy Spirit dwells within you and empowers your life so you can be used by the Lord. You will belong to Christ as His disciple (Ephesians 1:7-13).

These are the last days, not good days; it is an opportune time to place your confidence in Christ. Again, what path do you find yourself on? There is only one narrow gate—only one way! Can you truly commit your life to walk that narrow path sacrificially? It is never too late to change your eternal direction from being hell-bound to heaven-bound. May God speak to your heart.

14

SPIRITUAL DISCERNMENT

MATTHEW 7:15-23

In the Sermon on the Mount, Jesus gave His disciples a serious warning about false prophets. He exposed these men to be ravenous wolves disguised in sheep's clothing. Jesus knew His disciples would take the Gospel to the whole world, and it was necessary for them to have sound, spiritual discernment. Some of Jesus' disciples were hardworking fishermen. They had no formal seminary training, but they were privileged to be personally instructed by their Master—Jesus Christ.

In the book of Acts, when the rulers, elders, scribes, and even the High Priest heard Peter and John's address to the Sanhedrin, *they saw the boldness of Peter and John, and perceived that they were uneducated and untrained men, they marveled. And they realized that they had been with Jesus* (Acts 4:13).

WOLVES IN SHEEP'S CLOTHING — Matthew 7:15

"Beware of false prophets, who come to you in sheep's clothing, but inwardly they are ravenous wolves."

When Jesus warned His disciples about false prophets clothed in sheep's clothing, He was actually referring to the Pharisees, Sadducees and scribes. These religious leaders were an elite group of seventy-one elders who made up the Jewish court system—the Sanhedrin.

Most of the Jewish elders saw how the multitudes followed Jesus, and they became filled with jealousy and hatred. Murder filled their evil hearts. In an attempt to discourage the multitudes from following Jesus, they proclaimed to the people He was a false teacher and tried to ruin His perfect character.

Although these religious men had an in-depth knowledge of the Word of God and could easily quote from memory the Old Testament Scriptures, they really did not know God. They were far away from His kingdom. Being blind to spiritual truths themselves, they became blind guides to God's people.

Jesus revealed these religious leaders to be ravenous wolves in sheep's clothing. The word *ravenous* in the Greek language means "rapacious (excessively grasping or covetous), extortioners." They were supposed to be watching over God's people as shepherds, meek and mild as sheep among the people, but instead, they were wolves who tirelessly preyed on God's flock—exploiting and oppressing them. These Jewish leaders were outwardly devout, but inwardly they were full of pride and hypocrisy. In their actions, they certainly did not practice what they preached.

There have always been pastors and televangelists permeating social media platforms who are only interested in fleecing the flock for their own personal gain. When they preach, they subtly or blatantly ask for money. They exploit vulnerable widows and those who are ignorant in the Word. A preacher should never beg for funds. Any person professing to be a man called by God who places an emphasis on money in his messages signals to people that something is wrong. It is a sign that he is a false teacher.

Self-righteous, religious men who fleece the flock should be recognized as wolves in sheep's clothing. Like the pious Pharisees, Sadducees and scribes, they may have a lot of knowledge about the Bible, but most do not have a genuine relationship with Jesus Christ. They wear the outward garments of Christianity, but inwardly, as they are full of pride and hypocrisy, their actions will prove them to be otherwise.

Hudson Taylor became a most influential missionary to China. He received a call of God, and spent 51 years of his life in dedicated service to Christ. In the call of God, he never wanted support from the churches, but he went by faith, and God provided for every one of his needs. He wanted people to know, "Where the Lord leads, He provides." This is the philosophy of Calvary Chapel—"Where God guides, God provides." We do not ask for money, but trust in God. The Lord provides for those men who teach the Word of God genuinely, without hypocrisy.

Savage Wolves

The Apostle Paul continuously warned church leaders, those called to oversee God's flock, to be watchful for false teachers. Paul did so with tears because he knew the flock would not be spared:

> *"Therefore take heed to yourselves and to all the flock, among which the Holy Spirit has made you overseers, to shepherd the church of God which He purchased with His own blood. For I know this, that after my departure savage wolves will come in among you, not sparing the flock. Also from among yourselves men will rise up, speaking perverse things, to draw away the disciples after themselves. Therefore watch, and remember that for three years I did not cease to warn everyone night and day with tears."*

ACTS 20:28-31

Paul discerned that when he died, false shepherds would attack the flock of God, not from the outside, but from within the church. False teachers would approach believers who were weak in the faith—those not fully grounded in the Word of God. Leaders called to guard the flock should keep watch for those seeking to seduce the immature with their false philosophies that infect their minds and hearts.

Such was the case in the churches of Galatia. Believers were seduced into thinking they had to follow the Law to be saved. They were led astray into legalism and fell away from the grace of God. Paul stated the gravity of the situation and strictly warned: *But even if we, or an angel from heaven, preach any other gospel to you than what we have preached to you, let him be accursed* (Galatians 1:8).

The Greek word for *accursed* is the word *anathema*. It means "to be cursed—sent to the lowest hell." If false teachers tried to preach anything else other than grace—the unmerited favor given to us by God—Paul condemned them.

Any person who comes to Jesus by faith becomes a new creature (2 Corinthians 5:17). Salvation is by faith in Jesus Christ—period. A Christian is set free from the bondage of legalism, and by faith they rest in the finished work of Christ on the Cross (John 17:4). Oswald Chambers stated: "Every doctrine that is not embedded in the Cross of Jesus will lead astray."

Deceitful Workers

False teachers—deceitful workers—never get away with their deception. In the end, they will be judged. Listen to Paul's description of false apostles and the reference he gave to their just judgment:

> *For such are false apostles, deceitful workers, transforming themselves into apostles of Christ. And no wonder! For Satan himself transforms himself into an angel of light. Therefore it is no great thing if his ministers also transform themselves into ministers of righteousness, whose end will be according to their works.*

> 2 CORINTHIANS 11:13-15

The Apostle Peter also warned of false prophets and alluded to their swift destruction:

> *But there were also false prophets among the people, even as there will be false teachers among you, who will secretly bring in destructive heresies, even denying the Lord who bought them, and bring on themselves swift destruction. And many will follow their destructive ways, because of whom the way of truth will be blasphemed. By covetousness they will exploit you with deceptive words; for a long time their judgment has not been idle, and their destruction does not slumber.*
>
> 2 PETER 2:1-3

False prophets will ultimately fall under God's judgment if they do not repent.

Discerning False Doctrines

In the life of a Christian, it is necessary to have spiritual discernment. False teachers spread false doctrines. Ask God to give you the gift of discernment which will help you to recognize true doctrine from false doctrine. Believers cannot be ignorant of such lethal dangers. Embracing doctrines that are taught from false prophets and false teachers can lead a person to eternal destruction.

This short story can help people to think logically about the tragic consequences of someone believing in false information:

> I read about a lady and her young daughter who boarded a train journeying to the north. The woman was very concerned she would miss her stop and asked the conductor to please inform her when she arrived at her destination. The conductor promised he would let her know when she reached her journey's end. At first the lady completely relaxed, but as her trip continued, she became more anxious. A passenger

observed her anxiety and reassured her that conductors are very busy; the man was sure to be back soon to tell her when to exit the train.

However, after they passed more stops, and in the conductor's absence, the passenger took it upon himself to tell the concerned woman, "Do not worry; I will let you know when you are to get off the train." The passenger told the mother she had at last, finally arrived. Grateful, the mother took the hand of her daughter and exited the train. The thoughtful passenger observed them as they stood outside in the freezing cold. They watched the train leave the station and move slowly away into the distance.

Soon after, the conductor returned. He was surprised to see empty seats where the lady and her daughter were sitting. He asked the passenger seated near them if he had seen where they went. Confidently, the passenger told the conductor that, in his absence, he had informed the lady and daughter they had arrived at their stop instead. Both mother and daughter had safely exited the train at the last stop. The conductor was immediately troubled and exclaimed, "No! No! That was the wrong stop!" The well-meaning passenger had given them the wrong information!

The conductor quickly ordered the engine driver to slowly reverse backward down the track to try to find them. Sadly, it was too late; the mother and daughter had frozen to death in the snow. The false information given to them by the well-meaning passenger proved to be deadly.

The mother and daughter listened to a passenger rather than the conductor who knew exactly where their stop was. Think of how many people ignorantly accept false information as a true way of salvation. They simply believe in false teachings and false doctrines—a false gospel. False teachers will harm a person eternally.

The only way for salvation is to repent and believe by faith in Jesus Christ. People who believe this will safely arrive at an eternal, heavenly destination. However, those deceived into accepting a false gospel tragically will end up separated from God for all eternity, because they chose to believe a lie instead of the truth.

Test the Spirits

Some people identify themselves as Christians, but they actually belong to cults, such as: Christian Science, Mormonism, or Jehovah's Witnesses. Those who have embraced such false doctrines will often dispute the deity of Christ.

The Apostle John gave us a sure way to discern false doctrines. The infallible proof of a doctrine is to question the belief of Christ coming in human flesh:

> *Beloved, do not believe every spirit, but test the spirits, whether they are of God; because many false prophets have gone out into the world. By this you know the Spirit of God: Every spirit that confesses that Jesus Christ has come in the flesh is of God, and every spirit that does not confess that Jesus Christ has come in the flesh is not of God.*

1 JOHN 4:1-3

Abide in Christ's Doctrine

These deceptive doctrines also preach a message of works. They try to take young believers in Christ away from the truth. They believe they can get to heaven through works—Jesus plus something else. Not so! These deadly doctrines are taught by people who are false teachers. Be careful of them!

Jesus is in our hearts; Satan is in the world! Satan hates Christians. He will try to lead astray new believers, those who have just come to know Christ. Again, the immature Christian has not fully learned the Word of God, and they do not know how to defend themselves scripturally. Once they grow in Christ and develop spiritually, Satan will have a harder time in his attempts to deceive them.

The Apostle John warned about deceivers in the world and repeated a solid way to discern false doctrine from the doctrine of Christ:

> *For many deceivers have gone out into the world who do not confess Jesus Christ as coming in the flesh. This is a deceiver and an antichrist. Look to yourselves, that we do not lose those things we worked for, but that we may receive a full reward. Whosoever transgresses and does not abide in the doctrine of Christ does not have God. He who abides in the doctrine of Christ has both the Father and the Son. If anyone comes to you and does not bring this doctrine, do not receive him into your house nor greet him; for he who greets him shares in his evil deeds.*

2 JOHN 7-11

That is why it is important to study the Word of God. Yet how many Christians fail to bring their Bibles to church? We are a Bible-teaching church! You need your Bible when you come to Calvary Chapel! Open your Bible and mark down Scriptures so you can share the Gospel with a nonbeliever or those family members that might be ensnared in false doctrine.

Many Christians have not read through the entire Bible. How are they going to defend themselves from false teachers and false doctrine? Learn the Word of God so you can defend the Gospel biblically. When you rightly divide the Word of truth (2 Timothy 2:15), you will be able to discern a counterfeit doctrine when it is presented to you.

The doctrine of Jesus Christ is simple. A child can understand it. Jesus came, He died for our sins, and He resurrected from the dead—that is the Gospel. The Apostle Paul, a well-versed theologian, declared the Gospel simply:

> *Moreover, brethren, I declare to you the gospel which I preached to you, which also you received and in which you stand, by which also you are saved, if you hold fast that word which I preached to you—unless you believed in vain. For I delivered to you first of all that which I also received: that Christ died for our sins according to the Scriptures, and that He was buried, and that He rose again the third day according to the Scriptures....*

1 CORINTHIANS 15:1-4

So simple!

FRUIT INSPECTORS — Matthew 7:16-20

> "You will know them by their fruits. Do men gather grapes from thorn-bushes or figs from thistles? Even so, every good tree bears good fruit, but a bad tree bears bad fruit. A good tree cannot bear bad fruit nor can a bad tree bear good fruit. Every tree that does not bear good fruit is cut down and thrown into the fire. Therefore by their fruits you will know them."

Jesus revealed to us the way to discern a true Christian. He gave a clear distinction between a genuine Christian and someone who only professed Christianity. Jesus spoke straightforwardly and understandably using perfect illustrations of the impossibility of gathering healthy fruit from thorns, thistles and rotten trees, as opposed to gathering fruit from its own natural, healthy origin. Let us be realistic and use common sense— every natural tree yields its own fruit. A pear tree naturally bears pears, and an apple tree naturally bears apples. So just as we do not gather grapes from thorn-bushes or figs from thistles, a true Christian can be recognized by his spiritually fruitful life.

Even so, can a good tree bear bad fruit or a bad tree bear good fruit? The answer is obviously no! That just would not happen! Every person bears either good spiritual fruit or bad fruit in their lives.

There are those who say they are Christians, but they are false. We have to be able to identify a true Christian from those who just profess Christianity. Again, what do believers need to look for as evidence? Jesus gave us the answer: *"Therefore by their fruits you will know them"* (Matthew 7:20). Examine the fruit!

Christians have been called to be fruit inspectors. God will give discernment to those who ask Him for it. Using godly discernment as a believer, closely inspect the visible fruit in someone's life; then you will be able to easily judge the real Christians from those who are fake.

The Genuine Fruit of Love

What is the true spiritual fruit to be found in a Christian's life? It is the love of Jesus Christ. Christians have the natural fruit of love. If a person loves God, then they are going to demonstrate love toward others. The Holy Spirit has empowered them to do so. Therefore, love is the main evidence of the Holy Spirit working in and through their lives. Christ's love seen in the life of a true Christian identifies a genuine evidence of Christian fruitfulness.

Christians who obey God's Word will make a practice of loving other people. They exhibit an unconditional Christ-like love which continually lifts up others:

> *Love suffers long and is kind; love does not envy; love does not parade itself, is not puffed up; does not behave rudely, does not seek its own, is not provoked, thinks no evil; does not rejoice in iniquity, but rejoices in the truth; bears all things, believes all things, hopes all things, endures all things. Love never fails.*

> 1 CORINTHIANS 13:4-8

Christians can identify the natural fruit of a true Christian—Christ-likeness. Other natural fruits of the Spirit will also be seen in their lives: ...*the fruit of the Spirit is love, joy, peace, longsuffering, kindness, goodness, faithfulness, gentleness, self-control* (Galatians 5:22-23). The spiritual fruits they bear will testify of their true nature. Those who truly belong to God worship Him in Spirit and in truth (John 4:24). They follow the guidelines in the Word of God on how to obediently follow Jesus. The Word of God instructs believers what to do and what not to do. A true Christian will know in their heart when they are choosing to do something wrong—the Holy Spirit convicts them and they repent!

However, if there is no evidence of spiritual fruit in the life of a person who professes to be a Christian, then you would have to question their validity. If no fruit of the Spirit is detected, this person's life obviously does not match up with what they are saying. They have become a walking contradiction. Be on guard with this person.

Sin is manifested in a person's life bearing bad fruit. The evidence of the works of the flesh is listed in Galatians 5:19-21:

> *Now the works of the flesh are evident, which are: adultery, fornication, uncleanness, lewdness, idolatry, sorcery, hatred, contentions, jealousies, outbursts of wrath, selfish ambitions, dissensions, heresies, envy, murders, drunkenness, revelries, and the like; of which I tell you beforehand, just as I also told you in time past, that those who practice such things will not inherit the kingdom of God.*

You can now discern someone who is bearing bad fruit instead of good. Notice the end result of these sinful practices. They will not inherit the kingdom of God! If anyone professed to be a Christian and yet practiced sin, walking in constant disobedience to God's Word, they would not enter into the kingdom of God.

Jesus warned, "*Every tree that does not bear good fruit is cut down and thrown into the fire*" (Matthew 7:19). Many of you have different trees in your backyard—some lemon or orange trees. When you begin to see some of the branches are dying, and they are no longer bearing fruit, you trim the tree and take away the dry, dead branches. Many people use them as fuel to burn in their fires.

Jesus was referring to those souls who would be cast into the Lake of Fire. Yet Jesus never intended for people to go to hell. In fact, He said that hell was prepared for the devil and his angels (Matthew 25:41).

It is important to examine your own fruit, good or bad, because ultimately it reveals whether you will enter the kingdom of Heaven or not. John Blanchard stated: "A fruitless person is not a failed Christian, but a false one —in other words, not a Christian at all."

What kind of fruit are you bearing in your life?

ENTERANCE INTO THE KINGDOM OF HEAVEN
— Matthew 7:21

"Not everyone who says to Me, 'Lord, Lord,' shall enter the kingdom of heaven, but he who does the will of My Father in heaven."

All those who gathered to Jesus listened to Him intently. He spoke truth, plain and simple. The truth Jesus told them was that not everyone who called Him Lord would enter into the kingdom of heaven. Some people will say, "*Lord, Lord,*" but Jesus will declare to them, "*I never knew you.*" What had Jesus required of them in life? Obedience! Doing the will of God on earth made the difference eternally.

There is no real security to enter into the kingdom of God unless a person has truly accepted Christ as Lord and Savior. Why? True Christians continually abide in Jesus' love and walk in obedience to

God's Word (John 15). They are the ones who are truly doing the will of God.

I believe with all my heart, people can be very sincere in what they believe. They may feel that what they are doing is a just service to God, but they can be completely wrong. Those who speak religious words, but live sinful lives, are failing to do the will of God. They are, in fact, self-deceived. They must heed Jesus' warning!

Please, I urge you; take a good examination of your life. Have you been born again by God's Spirit, or are you just a religious person? Are you truly walking in obedience and doing the will of God?

I NEVER KNEW YOU! — Matthew 7:22-23

> "Many will say to Me [Jesus] in that day, 'Lord, Lord, have we not prophesied in Your name, cast out demons in Your name, and done many wonders in Your name?' And then I will declare to them, 'I never knew you; depart from Me, you who practice lawlessness!' "

Jesus gave such a stern warning to those listening to Him. He knew that religious people who exercised the gift of prophesy, cast out demons, and performed miracles would not make it into heaven. Even though they had performed all these miraculous things, they also habitually practiced sin.

There are people who may know how to speak spiritual words and even do miraculous works in Jesus' name, but they live their lives in rebellion—sinful disobedience. In judgment, Jesus would announce to them, *"I never knew you; depart from Me, you who practice lawlessness!"*

Again, notice the problem. Despite an outward show of Christianity, these people practiced lawlessness—sin. On close examination, their lives never matched up to what the Bible taught. Instead, they chose to live lives of sin. They never had changed lives.

Seriously, they will not make it into the kingdom of God, and they will perish because of their sin. I believe it could be possible that they were never in the kingdom of God to begin with! The Scriptures are clear—it is only the few who will make it into heaven:

> *"Enter by the narrow gate; for wide is the gate and broad is the way that leads to destruction, and there are many who go in by it. Because narrow is the gate and difficult is the way which leads to life, and there are few who find it."*

> MATTHEW 7:13-14

Jesus' warning applies to each of us. Are you living a life of disobedience to God's Word? Contemplate these convicting Scripture verses and honestly ask yourself where you stand spiritually:

> *Do you not know that the unrighteous will not inherit the kingdom of God? Do not be deceived. Neither fornicators, nor idolaters, nor adulterers, nor homosexuals, nor sodomites, nor thieves, nor covetous, nor drunkards, nor revilers, nor extortioners will inherit the kingdom of God.*

> 1 CORINTHIANS 6:9-10

There are those who genuinely think they are going to heaven, but, in reality, they are not. Those practicing sin will never be received into the Kingdom of Light.

Another exhortative and convicting poem is inscribed inside Lübeck Cathedral in Germany. It should be carefully taken to heart:

"Thus speaketh Christ our Lord to us:
Ye call Me Master and obey Me not.
Ye call Me Light and see Me not.
Ye call Me Way and walk Me not.
Ye call Me Life and choose Me not.
Ye call Me Wise and follow Me not.
Ye call Me Fair and love Me not.
Ye call Me Rich and ask Me not.
Ye call Me Eternal and seek Me not.
Ye call Me Noble and serve Me not.
Ye call Me Gracious and trust Me not.
Ye call Me Might and honor Me not.
Ye call Me Just and fear Me not.
If I condemn you, blame Me not."

You cannot call yourself a Christian and live in sin. It is imperative to turn from your sin before it is too late. None of us are guaranteed tomorrow. If you truly repent, God will forgive and cleanse you of your sin:

If we confess our sins, He is faithful and just to forgive us our sins and to cleanse us from all unrighteousness. If we say that we have not sinned, we make Him a liar, and His word is not in us.

1 JOHN 1:9-10

What happens when you turn from your sin? Jesus will wash, sanctify and justify you in His name and by the Spirit of God (1 Corinthians 6:11).

15

ROCK SOLID

MATTHEW 7:24-29

Jesus began a final discourse to conclude His great Sermon on the Mount. He started by saying, *therefore*, and, by using this term, Jesus took His disciples back to everything He had previously taught them. They were to remember all the incredible truths He had communicated to them in this heart-felt sermon.

Jesus had instructed His followers on how to be disciples of Christ, but now, in their commitment to Him, He encouraged them to exercise wisdom in applying everything they had learned. Practically, they needed to be doers of the Word, not hearers only. Through His wise words, Jesus would empower them to do the things He had taught them.

DOERS OF THE WORD — Matthew 7:24-27

"Therefore whoever hears these sayings of Mine, and does them, I will liken him to a wise man who built his house on the rock: And the rain descended, the floods came, and the winds blew and beat on that house; and it did not fall, for it was founded on the rock. But everyone who hears these sayings of Mine, and does not do them, will be like a foolish man who built his house on the sand: and the rain descended, the floods came, and the winds blew and beat on that house; and it fell. And great was its fall."

Jesus knew His disciples needed to have the right foundation in life. They were to build their lives on a good foundation—on the Rock. Who is the Rock? Jesus Christ! Going back to the time when the children of Israel were in the wilderness in 1 Corinthians 10:4, the Apostle Paul used the name Rock referring to Christ: *For they drank of that spiritual Rock that followed them, and that Rock was Christ.* Jesus Christ is the foundation on which the disciples were to *build their houses*—their lives on Him!

In giving understanding to His teaching, Jesus gave a compelling comparison between two builders—a wise man who built his house on the rock and a foolish man who built his house on the sand. When the storms of life came, the wise man had not only heard God's Word, but he had wisely applied to his life the biblical principles he had learned—his house stood.

However, the foolish person who built his house on the sand was not prepared for the storms of life. When the rain descended, and the floods and winds came, he had failed to apply God's Word to his life, so his house did not endure the storms of life—it fell. Using this simple illustration, Jesus once again revealed who the true believers really were. The evidence was seen when a person's life was tested. Did they stand or fall?

A Wise Builder

When a piece of land is purchased with the intent to build a home, the buyer makes sure it will be built on a solid foundation. He will check the ground to make sure the home can withstand any environmental hazards, such as earthquakes, floods or any other natural disasters.

When you consider that Christ is the Cornerstone of the Church (Ephesians 2:19-22), and that according to God's grace, our lives are built on that premise alone, we have a strong foundation that can withstand any storm: *For no other foundation can anyone lay than that which is laid, which is Jesus Christ* (1 Corinthians 3:11). Your life and the works you do are to be founded solely upon Christ.

If Jesus is the Rock of your life, your foundation, then nothing will remove you from your steadfastness. As you continue to obey the Word of God, when the storms of life come, the winds, floods and the rains that descend upon your house—they bring great trials, temptations and sicknesses, but nothing will move you. Your life will stand solid on the Rock.

Christian parents who are committed to Christ can prepare for whatever storms may take place in their homes and families. If children do not see their parents build their house on the Rock, then how are they going to see them stand? That is why parents have to read the Word of God and apply it. In times of great trial, they can immediately lean and stand upon the Scriptures. As they place their full trust in Christ, they are assured of His divine care. This becomes a great witness to their children.

Anyone who builds their life on Christ does not have to worry about anything. No matter what storms you are going through, know that He will uphold you. Christ will give you an unshakable assurance that life will be all right after the storm passes.

Wise Christians will continually examine and strengthen the structures of their homes, as they can run into problems. The windows or doors may have warped, and they do not fit right, the roof may need fixing, or expensive plumbing may need to be installed—whatever it is.

It is wise to examine the foundation of your life. Is it built on the Rock or the sand? If sand, then how will you change the way you are building?

A Foolish Builder

When you go up to Jerusalem, which is 2000 feet above sea level, and then look toward the Dead Sea, you will see that when the rain pours, the water has only one place to go—into the desert. In times past, people built their homes on this unstable, sandy area.

Sand is nothing more than fine, little grains of rock and minerals. As the ocean waves hit the rocks, little pebbles are formed, and eventually they become sand. Imagine, sand particles are so small that it is impossible to count them; they are far too numerous. Sand is an unstable, moveable foundation; it easily washes away. When sudden storms rage and rains descend, gaps will develop under the foundations of homes built on sand. They will be completely swept away because the foundation was not built on rock.

There are many who hear the Gospel of Jesus Christ, but never obey it—they never learn. So during stormy trials, they are devastated. When nonbelievers go through a difficult trial, they often start to curse God and blame Him for everything. They raise a clenched fist at God. They do not know God or the Scriptures; they cannot fully understand the grace, mercy and sovereignty of God. Those who do not know God fail to have a rock-solid foundation; they lack Christ's assurance to see them through the trials of life.

Even within the Church, you will find carnal people who are living according to their fleshly desires. Like the nonbeliever, they do not have a solid foundation—their life is built on the sand. It is of no value for a single soul to sit among the congregation and hear the Word of God when they have no intention of obeying Jesus' teachings.

Biblical principles have to be applied; then a person becomes wise. People who deliberately reject Christ's words are foolish. They do not pay attention, and they do not obey. These people have a false security. Needless to say, when the storms of life suddenly hit, bringing torrential rains, floods and winds, what is going to happen? During the storms of life, they will not have a stable foundation; they will be demolished and swept away with the floods. They are not anchored to the Rock, so they cannot withstand the trials of life. They are truly likened to the man who has built his house on sand, *"and the rain descended, the floods came, and the winds blew and beat on that house; and it fell. And great was its fall."*

Jesus closed His sermon with a call to obedience—to life embedded in the Rock. Truly, truly, if you want to go into the kingdom of God, then build your house on the Rock; otherwise, if your house is built on the sand, you are going to slip away—you will be gone!

The Bedrock Faith of Job

Contemplate the bedrock faith of Job. In times of abundance and prosperity, as well as times of devastation and tragedy, his foundation remained solid. He remained immovable in his trust in God. Job went through an immense season of trial. God gave Satan permission to take all his wealth, his sons and his daughters, but Job never once falsely accused God: *Yet, in all this Job did not sin nor charge God with wrong* (Job 1:22). Could you and I do that?

Job continued to endure extreme pressure under his trial. Satan was given permission to afflict him. He was covered with boils from the top of his head to the bottom of his feet. He could not sit, lie down or walk. At one point, his wife, seeing Job's anguish, demanded: *"Do you still hold fast to your integrity? Curse God and die!"* Again, although greatly tested, listen to his reply: *"You speak as one of the foolish women speaks. Shall we indeed accept good from God, and shall we not accept adversity?" In all this Job did not sin with his lips* (Job 2:9-10).

Job's bedrock faith was grounded in the eternal perspective that he would one day see God. In actually this statement of Job prophetically pointed to the Resurrection of Christ:

> *"For I know that my Redeemer lives and He shall stand at last on the earth; and after my skin is destroyed, this I know, that in my flesh I shall see God, whom I shall see for myself, and my eyes shall behold, and not another. How my heart yearns within me!"*

> JOB 19:25-27

In times of severe trial, as Christians, we too shall be tried and tested! Many times, in a season of testings, we question God, asking, "Why is this happening to me?" Believers may be tempted to bring a false accusation against God.

As God's children, sometimes we have to go through affliction. As with Job, God may allow believers to suffer in order to accomplish His will and give Him glory. Again, like Job, it could be a demonic attack. Others go through suffering because they are reaping to their own foolishness—their sin. Believers will go through the fire of affliction, but these things help build their character and build a bedrock faith in Christ. Trials can be harsh, but they make us strong, and they give us compassion for other people. We pray endurance for those who are hurting, in pain and suffering infirmities.

Christians will face many trials in life, so it is important to know the Scriptures. As a true Christian, you will be able to endure trials because you are depending on Christ. Nothing will shake your faith! Not cancer, nor height nor demonic principalities—not even death! Why? Your life is stable; it is grounded upon the Rock Jesus Christ. This is bedrock faith!

The Tested and Tried Faith of Abraham

God came to Abraham to test him. The words *to test* mean "to try." Abraham was placed into the greatest test of his life! God asked Abraham to give up his son, his only son Isaac, the son of promise, on an altar of sacrifice at Mount Moriah (Genesis 22:1-2). God's intent was to test Abraham by proving his unconditional obedience to Him.

Remember, Abraham and Sarah had waited on the Lord to have a child until all possibility was gone. They had grown so old! Yet nothing was impossible for God. Even though Sarah was past the age of childbearing, at the age of 90 she conceived and bore a son, Isaac—meaning "laughter." Abraham was then 100 years old (Genesis 18:9-15; 21:1-6).

Abraham's faith rested in the faithful promise of God. The Lord had promised Abraham that he would become a father of many nations (Genesis 12:1-3). Now God would prove Abraham's faith by asking him to place his beloved son on the altar. From Genesis 21:34 to Genesis 22:1, at least 25 years had passed, and Isaac was now a young man.

In complete obedience to God, Abraham gathered his servants, the donkey, the wood and his knife, and, accompanied by his son, he prepared to take the three-day journey to Mount Moriah (Genesis 22:3-4). When they arrived, Abraham told his servants: *"Stay here with the donkey; the lad and I will go yonder and worship, and we will come back to you"* (Genesis 22:5). Notice, Abraham spoke of coming back to them. He believed that, even if he killed his son, God would be able to resurrect him. He had an unshakable faith in God. The word *worship* literally means in Hebrew "to bow down." Abraham was bending his will—to the will of God.

Abraham approached the place of sacrifice, Mount Moriah. He had laid the wood on his son Isaac, while he carried the fire and a knife in his hand (Genesis 22:6). Then Isaac respectfully asked his father an obvious question:

> *And Isaac spake unto Abraham his father, and said, My father: and he said, Here am I, my son. And he said, Behold the fire and the wood: but where is the lamb for a burnt offering? And Abraham said, My son, God will provide himself a lamb for a burnt offering: so they went both of them together.*

> GENESIS 22:7-8, KJV

Isaac would be the sacrifice! As they reached the place God had told Abraham, an altar was built. Isaac, in total submission, was bound by his father and laid on the altar upon the wood (Genesis 22:9). Right at the point when Abraham raised the knife to kill his son,

> *...the Angel of the LORD* [pre-existent Jesus Christ] *called to him from heaven and said, "Abraham, Abraham!" So he said, "Here I am." And He said, "Do not lay your hand on the lad, or do anything to him; for now I know that you fear God, since you have not withheld your son, your only son, from Me."*

GENESIS 22:11-12

Abraham passed the test—he did not withhold his son. Then seeing in the thicket a ram caught by its horns, Abraham offered the ram as a burnt sacrifice instead of his son (Genesis 22:13). In remembrance, *Abraham called the name of the place, The-LORD-Will-Provide; as it is said to this day, "In the Mount of the LORD it shall be provided"* (Genesis 22:14). God blessed Abraham and reaffirmed the promise that Abraham held on to during his time of testing:

> *"By Myself I have sworn, says the LORD, because you have done this thing, and have not withheld your son, your only son— blessing I will bless you, and multiplying I will multiply your descendants as the stars of the heaven and as the sand which is on the seashore; and your descendants shall possess the gate of their enemies. In your seed all the nations of the earth shall be blessed, because you have obeyed My voice."*

GENESIS 22:16-18

We have been affected by the promise given to Abraham, the promise of the Messiah to be born.

The journey to Mount Moriah is very significant, as there is a lot of typology found in Genesis 22. Abraham becomes a type of God the Father, who loves His Only Beloved Son. Isaac becomes a type of Jesus Christ, who the Father sent into the world. Abraham's son was probably about 33 year's old—the same age as Jesus Christ, who willingly went to the Cross for mankind. He submitted His will to the Father. Isaac carried the wood, which is a type of the Cross that Christ carried when He became the Lamb of God, the sacrifice for the sins of the world.

It reminds us of John 3:16: *"For God so loved the world that He gave His only begotten Son, that whoever believes in Him should not perish but have everlasting life."* The three-day journey becomes a type of the Resurrection! Jesus was in the grave, and then He rose on the third day!

Through this beautiful story, 2000 years before it happened, is seen a vivid picture of how God provided His Son for the sacrifice! Jesus the Messiah would be crucified on the same Mount Moriah, which today is called "the Mount of the Skull." How much God loves us!

Abraham returned to the young men (Genesis 22:19), but it is interesting that Isaac was not mentioned until Genesis 24, when he married Rebecca. They became a part of Christ's bloodline—a family's faith was built on the Rock!

Like Abraham, every Christian will come to a place of enduring a great trial in life. During a trial, know God will give you the power to overcome. Hold on to the faithful promises of God. In the midst of a stormy trial, what specific promises has God given to you that you can now reflect upon? His promises are foundational to your Christian faith.

God has His reasons for allowing a test to come into your life. Often it is to prove, mold and shape your character. A test will prove your obedience. Will you obey or disobey Him? How can He trust you with a task if you are not faithful or obedient to Him?

When you are tried and tested, God will see your genuine faith. Do you trust Him? Is there anything in this life that you would withhold from Him? What or who is your Isaac? What is God asking you to place on the altar? Have you bowed your will to the will of God?

It is important to fear God, reverence Him because it is in His power to bless and reward you exceedingly. As with Abraham and Isaac, God has a great work for you to fulfill.

Peter's Imbedded Faith at Pentecost

Jesus had called a common, rugged fisherman to follow Him. At times, Peter was very zealous, even spiritually perceptive, but he was also self-confident. He received both praise and rebuke from his Master. Peter loved the Lord he followed.

At a region called Caesarea Philippi, a place where there is a big rock and where many false gods were worshipped, Jesus questioned His disciples, saying, *"Who do men say that I, the Son of Man, am?"* He received varied answers from His disciples. Then, Jesus asked: *"But who do you say that I am?"* Simon Peter had a spiritual revelation and boldly declared: *"You are the Christ, the Son of the living God"* (Matthew 16:13, 15-16).

Then Jesus said to Peter:

> *"Blessed are you, Simon Bar-Jonah, for flesh and blood has not revealed this to you, but My Father who is in heaven. And I also say to you that you are Peter, and on this rock I will build My church, and the gates of Hades shall not prevail against it."*

> MATTHEW 16:17

According to the Scriptures, Peter would be known in the Greek as *petros* meaning "a small, little stone;" in distinction, Christ is the Rock— *petra*—and on this "massive stone," He would build His Church. Jesus is the Rock—the Cornerstone of the Church (Ephesians 2:19-20). Even though Peter had this revelation of Christ, his life's foundation would be intensely tested. Would his foundation be founded upon sinking sand or on the sure foundation of the Rock?

Jesus, knowing all things, knew Satan had asked to sift Peter's life as wheat:

> *And the Lord said, "Simon, Simon! Indeed, Satan has asked for you, that he may sift you as wheat. But I have prayed for you, that your faith should not fail; and when you have returned to Me, strengthen your brethren."*

> LUKE 22:31-32

Jesus had already prayed for His zealous disciple. At Christ's arrest in the Garden of Gethsemane, in misdirected zeal, Peter persisted in relying on his own strength to defend the Lord; he pulled out his sword and cut of the ear of the High Priest's servant. Jesus healed him, and at His word, Peter placed his sword back into its sheath—he put away his weapon. Peter was shaken, bewildered and afraid. Peter forsook his Lord and ran.

Even though at one time Peter had zealously said to Jesus: *"Even if I have to die with You, I will not deny You!"* (Matthew 26:35). The disciples all scattered, but Peter followed as close as he could to the trial, and found himself in the courtyard of the High Priest, warming himself by the enemies' fire. When questioned whether he was a follower of Christ or not, he denied the Lord three times. Failure after failure must have troubled his mind. Peter's weary eyes met the penetrating eyes of his tortured Master. The second crow of a rooster pierced the early dawn. Only then did Peter call to mind the words of Jesus: *"Before the rooster crows twice, you will deny Me three times."* Peter broke down and wept in true repentance (Mark 14:66-72).

Although Peter had a time of great weakness as his faith was tested, through the intercessory prayers of Christ, he was strengthened. He returned to serve Christ, and although his foundation had been shaken, it was not destroyed. Humility and repentance helped him to rebuild and fortify his foundation—no longer would he depend upon himself. His life was fully imbedded in the One who was forever fixed as the Rock of the Church—Jesus Christ. There could be no other foundation.

After the Resurrection, Jesus recommissioned Peter—*feed my sheep* (John 21:17). On the Day of Pentecost, strengthened in his faith, an emboldened Peter stood unmovable and unshakable in the presence of men. Unafraid and full of the Holy Spirit's power, the Gospel was theologically explained. Peter preached with authority—the authority of Christ. Cut to the heart, over three thousand souls came to Christ that day (Acts 2:14-41).

On another occasion, Peter with John, after healing a lame man in the name of Jesus, boldly preached on the Resurrection of Christ, and about five thousand believed. Arrested and questioned by the rulers of the people and elders of Israel, their boldness was witnessed. These leaders concluded:...*they were uneducated and untrained men, they marveled...* (Acts 4:13). Noticeably, Peter, a mere, uneducated fisherman, had been with Jesus—the Rock of his salvation.

We all have been like Peter—self-confident, foolishly building our lives on the sand. Yet Jesus has prayed for each one of us: *"I pray for them* [believers]. *I do not pray for the world but for those whom You have given Me, for they are Yours"* (John 17:9). All of us at one time or another have had to repent of our foolishness and for denying Christ, either by our actions or words. Jesus strengthens us so our lives can be rebuilt on the Rock.

Is your life fully imbedded in Christ? Can people tell you have been with Jesus? Have they witnessed the power and authority of Christ in your actions and words?

CHRIST'S AUTHORITY — Matthew 7:28-29

> And so it was, when Jesus had ended these sayings, that the people were astonished at His teaching, for He taught them as one having authority, and not as the scribes.

Jesus concluded the Sermon on the Mount with a final exhortation to be as the wise man—a doer of the Word and not a hearer only. As He ended these sayings, notice the reaction of the people who had heard Him speak. They were completely astonished at His teaching. They had never heard a teaching taught with such power and authority. The scribes, Pharisees and Sadducees preached to the people, but their words had no power, as they had never lived what they taught.

Jesus taught the people with such authority. His words were commanding and convicting. The hearts of many men and women were moved—a true transformation happened in the lives of all who chose to follow Him.

Think on the power and authority of Jesus' Words:

> *For the word of God is living and powerful, and sharper than any two-edged sword, piercing even to the division of soul and spirit, and of joints and marrow, and is a discerner of the thoughts and intents of the heart.*

> HEBREWS 4:12

All authority belongs to Jesus! He is all powerful. Jesus Himself declared: *"All authority has been given to Me in heaven and on earth"* (Matthew 28:18). Jesus Christ is all knowing, *in whom are hidden all the treasures of wisdom and knowledge* (Colossians 2:3).

Jesus is ever-present—everywhere at all times. Not only does Jesus see everything, He is among us, listening and watching: *"For where two or three are gathered together in My name, I am there in the midst of them"* (Matthew 18:20).

Jesus has always existed; He is eternal. Jesus is God— deity. He is the Word and was eternally with God in the beginning:

> *In the beginning was the Word, and the Word was with God, and the Word was God. He was in the beginning with God. All things were made through Him, and without Him nothing was made that was made.*

> JOHN 1:1-3

God the Father decided in eternity, before the earth was ever created, to send His Son to be born from a virgin, as a Babe. He spent 33 years in this hostile world. Mankind rejected Him and spit on Him. They placed on Christ a crown of thorns and crucified Him on the Cross.

They took down His bruised and battered body and buried Him, but on the third day, He rose from the dead. Jesus was taken up to heaven, but 50 days later, on the Day of Pentecost, the Holy Spirit descended (Acts 2:1-4).

Jesus' words remain with us. They are still relevant for us, His followers, to take to heart, to obey, and to make them a daily practice. I believe it is impossible to go through the Sermon on the Mount and not bring about change in our lives. The Holy Spirit will bring great conviction to our hearts because of the nature and purpose of God in transforming us to be Christ-like.

As you have spent considerable time studying and contemplating *The Sermon of Sermons, Christ's Sermon on the Mount,* with the beautiful Beatitudes, have you been astonished at Christ's teachings? In His authority, how has Jesus spoken to you, personally?

I pray these incredible insights cause you to search your heart, and give you a greater passion to serve the Lord Jesus Christ for the rest of your mortal life!

SOMEBODY LOVES YOU PUBLISHING
WWW.SOMEBODYLOVESYOU.COM

BOOKS

Raul Ries

From Fury to Freedom
From Fury to Freedom***
Man: Natural, Carnal, Spiritual
Impurity: The Naked Truth
Sin: The Root of All Evil
Doctrines: A Simplified Road Map of Biblical Truth
Doctrines: A Simplified Road Map of Biblical Truth***
Servant: The Person God Uses
Victory: Overcoming the Enemy
Seven Steps to a Successful Marriage*
Seven Steps to a Successful Marriage***
Raising a Godly Family in an Ungodly World
Somebody Loves You Growth Book**
30 Questions that Deserve Answers**
Understanding God's Compassion**
Living Above Your Circumstances: A Study in the Book of Daniel
Hear What the Spirit Is Saying
Marriage: Vowed Inseparable
The Sermon of Sermons: Christ's Sermon on the Mount

Chuck Smith

Calvary Chapel—The Philosophy of Ministry*

Sharon Faith Ries

The Well-Trodden Path
My Husband, My Maker
The Night Cometh: Edmund and Naomi Farrel

Claire Wren

Crimson

STUDY MATERIALS

The Infinite God (23 studies)
*Women In His Image** (24 studies)
The Word Became Flesh (the book of John—23 studies)
*A Woman Who Fears The Lord** (Proverbs 31—10 studies)
*Old Testament Stories For Perilous Times** (11 studies)
The Acts of the Apostles (24 studies)
Genuine Faith: The Epistle of James (12 studies)
*Instructive Moments in the Old Testament** (inductive study)
*A Divine Appointment with the Savior** (inductive study)

DVDs

Raul Ries

*Fury to Freedom**
Taking the Hill: 2-DVD Package*
*A Quiet Hope**
*A Venture in Faith: The History and Philosophy of the
  Calvary Chapel Movement**

FILMS

Shane Ries

The Parisian Incident
Cycle
W 3sixty5
Abraham's Desert

Base 9
base9.com

*available in Spanish **booklet ***audio book

Somebody Loves You Publishing
22324 Golden Springs Drive
Diamond Bar, CA 91765-2449
(800) 634-9165
mail@somebodylovesyou.com
www.somebodylovesyou.com

Somebody Loves You Radio is the teaching ministry of Pastor Raul Ries. Since committing his life to Christ in 1972, Raul has been driven to share the message of God's love to a lost and dying world, on a 30-minute daily program which is heard worldwide on over 350 stations. It can also be accessed on the *Somebody Loves You* website, mobile app, and podcasts. The vision of *Somebody Loves You* is simple but powerful—to reach the world for Christ.

ENDNOTES

[1] Dietrich Bonhoeffer, The Cost of Discipleship (London: SCM Press, 2015), 118.

[2] A. W. Tozer, The Pursuit of God (Chicago: Moody Publishers, 2015).

[3] A. W. Tozer, The Best of A.W. Tozer, Book One (Camp Hill, PA: Wing Spread, 2007).

[4] Billy Graham, Billy Graham in Quotes (Nashville: Thomas Nelson, 2011).

[5] Arthur Wallis, God's Chosen Fast (Fort Washington, PA: CLC Publications, 1975), 43.

[6] Ibid., 43.

[7] Billy Graham, Angels/Peace with God (Nashville: Thomas Nelson, 2009).

[8] Dietrich Bonhoeffer, The Collected Sermons of Dietrich Bonhoeffer, Volume One (Minneapolis: Fortress Press, 2012).

[9] Dietrich Bonhoeffer, Bonhoeffer's The Cost of Discipleship (Nashville: B & H Publishing Group, 1999) 57.

[10] A. W. Tozer, The Root of the Righteous (Chicago: Moody Publishers, 2015).

[11] David Curry, Open Doors USA, "Open Doors to expose China's human rights nightmare at DC Press Conference on January 15," www.religionnews.com, (RNS Press Release, 1-13-2020).

[12] Billy Graham, The Reason for My Hope: Salvation (Nashville: Thomas Nelson, 2015) 128.